THIS IS THE
GARDEN

AN ANTHOLOGY
OF WRITERS IN GARDENS

THIS IS THE GARDEN

AN ANTHOLOGY
OF WRITERS IN GARDENS

Edited and Introduced by
Charles Elliott

F

FRANCES LINCOLN LIMITED
PUBLISHERS

Frances Lincoln Ltd
4 Torriano Mews
Torriano Avenue,
London NW5 2RZ
www.franceslincoln.com

First Frances Lincoln edition 2011

A catalogue record for this book is available
from the British Library

ISBN 978-0-7112-3174-0

Printed and bound in China

1 2 3 4 5 6 7 8 9

CONTENTS

Introduction 9

Romance 12

Garden Making 36

Enthusiasm 69

Far Away 91

Scepticism 105

Styles 123

Sinister 140

Intensities 153

Lost Gardens 169

Who's Who 180

Sources & Acknowledgments 192

Index 194

THIS IS THE GARDEN

this is the garden:colours come and go,
frail azure fluttering from night's outer wing
strong silent greens serenely lingering,
absolute lights like baths of golden snow.
This is the garden:pursèd lips do blow
upon cool flutes within wide glooms.and sing
(of harps celestial to the quivering string)
invisible faces hauntingly and slow.

This is the garden. Time shall surely reap
and on Death's blade lie many a flower curled,
in other lands, where other songs be sung:
yet stand They here enraptured,as among
the slow deep trees perpetual of sleep
some silver-fingered fountain steals the world.

e e cummings from *Chimneys and Tulips* (1923)

INTRODUCTION

Garden writing is a peculiar genre. Its annals are studded with remarkable practitioners, from Christopher Lloyd to Penelope Hobhouse to Henry Mitchell and Reginald Farrer. Most of these writers were serious gardeners in their own right, perfectly equipped not only to describe but to instruct. We may well read them to be amused, but we also read them because they can tell us what to do and how to do it. We read them to learn.

But there is another sort of writing about gardens. The aim of this anthology is to show how pervasive gardens are in the wider world of literature. Again and again, novelists, essayists and poets, whose own direct concern with gardening may be slight, find themselves deeply involved with particular gardens—using them as a setting, describing them, contemplating them, engaging with them metaphorically or as a way of expressing emotion. Thus gardens turn up in the most unlikely places, from the Russian countryside in Gogol to tenth century Japan in the *Pillow Book* of the court lady Sei Shōnagon, as well, of course, as the writing of many great English novelists.

The great majority of authors included here are not gardeners, although a few are, such as Sir George Sitwell, Alexander Pope and John Parkinson. But even those that aren't seem more than ordinarily sensitive to the moods gardens can evoke. Not that the moods are always favourable. Dr. Johnson could be scathing (and funny) about the poet William Shenstone's Leasowes ('rather the sport than the business of human reason' was his verdict on the practice of garden design), while Charlotte Brontë is chilled by the ghostly aura of a small Belgian park. Yet for every writer confounded by a garden there are many others dazzled or virtually overcome, like Virginia Woolf observing the mixture of colours in Kew Gardens, human and botanical, or Andrew Marvell stumbling through an orchard 'Insnar'd with Flow'rs.' That writers as widely divergent as Jerome K. Jerome and Goethe, Somerset Maugham and Homer—to say nothing of James I and Elizabeth Bowen—all brought gardens into their works says something about how gardens are a part of the lives of so many different kinds of people.

I've tried in this collection to keep to specifics; that is, to choose extracts from writers describing particular gardens which though often fictional are anything but vague or generic. What is significant about them, without exception, is that they are 'felt' gardens. They have touched the writers by their beauty or meaning or (in a few cases) their fearfulness. And the writers have in turn found surprising ways to make use of the gardens in their poems or stories, to express ecstasy, a state of placidity or terror, nostalgia or the passage of time.

Whatever the intention of the writers, however, what's really remarkable about this marriage between horticulture and literature is the extraordinary, even dazzling, variety of gardens that emerge from it. If anyone ever imagined that gardening was a simple one-note art, the descriptions included here should be enough to disabuse them. A prey neither to time nor weather, these gardens remain a testament to the power of imagination.

ROMANCE

The archtypical garden is a romantic garden, a place for dreams rather than reality. Everything in it is slightly heightened—the scents stronger, the shade deeper, the whole ensemble richer than anything you'd find in the ordinary world. Likewise, in fact especially, in literature. As a setting for strong emotions, what better place for imagination to roam than through the glades and avenues of a romantic garden?

Thus a novelist like the extraordinary Benjamin Disraeli, prime minister and dandy, politician and storyteller, luxuriates in the slightly overwrought splendours of a castle garden, while a real king, James I of Scotland, looks to his own royal garden to assuage his sadness. In neither case is there an attempt at literal description; all is bedazzled. Henry James in *The Awkward Age* places his young heroine in the grand park of an English country house; we feel both the girl's pleasure and bemusement and James's own. Sometimes, of course, the romance is less in nature of the garden than the intensity of observation the writer brings to it—Marcel Proust in the Bois de Boulogne is an exquisite example—or the romantic activities that tend to go on there. For delicate eroticism, it would be difficult to match Colette writing about a boy and a girl and a slug in a dripping wet Parisian garden. And that too is romance.

Benjamin Disraeli
Henrietta Temple (1836)

Armine Place, before Sir Ferdinand, unfortunately for his descendants, determined in the eighteenth century on building a feudal castle, had been situate in famous pleasure-grounds, which extended at the back of the mansion over a space of some hundred acres. The grounds in the immediate vicinity of the buildings had of course suffered severely, but the far greater portion had only been neglected, and there were some indeed who deemed, as they wandered through the arbour-walks of this enchanting wilderness, that its beauty had been enhanced even by this very neglect. It seemed like a forest in a beautiful romance, a green and bowery wilderness where Boccaccio would have loved to woo, and Watteau to paint. So artfully had the walks been planned, that they seemed interminable, nor was there a single point in the whole pleasaunce where the keenest eye could have detected a limit. Sometimes you wandered in those arched and winding walks dear to pensive spirits, sometimes you emerged on a plot of turf blazing in the sunshine, a small and bright savannah, and gazed with wonder on the group of black and mighty cedars that rose from its centre, with their sharp and spreading foliage. The beautiful and the vast blended together; and the moment after you had beheld with delight a bed of geraniums or of myrtles, you found yourself in an amphitheatre of Italian pines. A strange exotic perfume filled the air; you trod on the flowers of other lands; and shrubs and plants, that usually are only trusted from their conservatories, like sultanas from their jalousies, to sniff the air and recall their bloom, here learning from hardship the philosophy of endurance, had struggled successfully even against northern winters, and wantoned now in native and unpruned luxuriance. Sir Ferdinand, when he resided at Armine, was accustomed to fill these pleasure-grounds with macaws and other birds of gorgeous plumage, but these had fled away with their master, all but some swans which still floated on the surface of a lake, which marked the centre of this paradise. In the remains of the ancient seat of his fathers, Sir Ratcliffe Armine and his bride now sought a home.

*

Honoré de Balzac
Beatrix (1839)

The garden is magnificent for so old a place. It covers half an acre of ground, its walls are all espaliered, and the space within is divided into squares for vegetables, bordered with cordons of fruit-trees, which the man-of-all-work, named Gasselin, takes care of in the intervals of grooming the horses. At the farther end of the garden is a grotto with a seat in it; in the middle, a sun-dial; the paths are gravelled. The façade on the garden side has no towers corresponding to those in the court-yard; but a slender spiral column rises from the ground to the roof, which must in former days have borne the banner of the family, for at its summit may be seen an iron socket, from which a few weak plants are straggling. This detail, in harmony with the vestiges of sculpture, proves to a practiced eye that the mansion was built by a Venetian architect. The graceful staff is like a signature revealing Venice, chivalry, and the exquisite delicacy of the thirteenth century. If any doubts remained on this point, a feature of the ornamentation would dissipate them. The trefoils of the hotel de Guaisnic have four leaves instead of three. This difference plainly indicates the Venetian school depraved by its commerce with the East, where the semi-Saracenic architects, careless of the great Catholic thought, give four leaves to clover, while Christian art is faithful to the Trinity. In this respect Venetian art becomes heretical.

*

Robert Heath
"On Clarastella Walking in Her Garden" from *Clarastella* (1650)

See how *Flora* smiles to see
This approaching Deitie!
Where each herb looks young and green
In the presence of their coming Queen!
Ceres with all her fragrant store
Could never boast so sweet a flow'r;
While thus in triumph she doth go
The greater Goddess of the two.
Here the Violet bows to greet
Her with homage to her feet;
There the Lilly pales with white
Got by her reflexed light;
Here a Rose in crimson dye
Blushes through her modestie;
There a Pansie hangs his head
'Bout to shrink into his bed
'Cause so quickly she pass'd by

Not returning suddenly;
Here the Currants red and white
In yon green bush at her sight
Peep through their shady leaves, and cry
Come eat me, as she passes by;
There a bed of Camomile,
When she presseth it doth smell
More fragrant than the perfum'd East,
Or the *Phoenix* spicie nest;
Here the Pinks in rows do throng
To guard her as she walks along.
There the flexive Turnsole bends
Guided by the rayes she sends
From her bright eyes, as if from thence
It suckt life by influence;
While She, the prime and chiefest flow'r
In all the garden by her pow'r
And onely life-inspiring breath
Like the warm Sun redeems from death
Their drooping heads, and bids them live
To tell us She their sweets did give.

*

Colette

The Innocent Libertine (1904–05)
Translated by Antonia White

She ran out into the still dripping garden, followed by
Antoine, trailing sulkily behind her. She ran along the still
soaking paths, gazing at the rejuvenated garden. In the
distance, the ridge of the mountains steamed like the back of

an over-driven horse and the earth was drinking in the last drops in a pullulating silence.

In front of the Venetian Sumac, known in France as a 'peruque tree', Minne stopped dead, dazzled. It was as rosy and ornate and vaporous as the sky on a Trianon ceiling. The dappled clouds of its hair sparkled with diamond raindrops; she would not have been surprised to see naked Cupids, the kind that hold festoons of blue ribbon and have too much vermilion on their cheeks and behinds, fly up out of it.

The espalier was dripping, but the lemon-shaped peaches known as 'Venus breasts' had stayed warm and dry under their painted waterproof velvet. The roses were heavy with rain, and so that she could shake them Minne had turned back her sleeves, displaying slim ivory arms, iridescent with a down even paler than her hair. Antoine watched her morosely, biting his lips at the thought that he could kiss those arms, feel that silver down caress his mouth.

Now she was squatting down over a red slug, the delicate tips of her curls trailing in a puddle.

'Look, Antoine, how red and grainy it is—just like a leather handbag.'

He did not deign to bend his head and his big nose remained sulkily stuck in the air.

'Antoine, please turn it over. I want to see if it'll be fine tomorrow.'

'How?'

'It was Célénie who told me: if slugs have earth on the ends of their noses, it's a sign of fine weather.'

'Turn it over yourself!'

'No, slugs are disgusting.'

Grumbling so as preserve his dignity, Antoine turned the

slug over with a twig. It dribbled and contracted itself. Minne was very attentive.

'Which end is its nose?'

*

James I of Scotland
The Kingis Quair (ca. 1423)

Bewailing in my chamber thus alone,
Despeired of all Joye and remedye,
Fortyred of my thought, and woe begone,
Unto the window gan I walk in hye,
To see the warld and folk that went forbye;
As for the tyme, though I of mirthis fude *happiness bereft*
Myght have no more, to look it did me gude.
Now there was made fast by the tower's wall
A gardyn faire, and in the corners set
An arbour grene, with wandis long and small   *walks*
Railed about; and so with treis set
Was all the place, and hawthorn hedges knit,
That lyf was none walking there forbye,
That myght within scarce any wight espy.   *see anyone*
So thick the bewis and the leavis greene   *boughs*
Beshaded all the alleys that there were,
And myddis every arbour might be seen   *midst*
The sharp, greene, sweete Juniper
Growing so faire with branches here and there,
That, as It semyt to a lyf without,
The bewis spred the arbour all about;
And on the small, greene twistis sat   *twigs*

19

The lytill sweet nightingale, and sung
So loud and clere, the ympnis consecrate   *hymns*
Of lufis use, now soft, now lowd among   *love's*
That all the gardyn and the wallis rung   *walls*
Ryght of thaire song...

*

L. M. Montgomery
Anne of Green Gables (1908)

But it was morning and, yes, it was a cherry-tree in full
bloom outside of her window. With a bound she was out of
bed and across the floor. She pushed up the sash—it went
up stiffly and creakily, as if it hadn't been opened for a long
time, which was the case; and it stuck so tight that nothing
was needed to hold it up.

Anne dropped on her knees and gazed out into the June
morning, her eyes glistening with delight. Oh, wasn't it
beautiful? Wasn't it a lovely place? Suppose she wasn't really
going to stay here! She would imagine she was. There was
scope for imagination here.

A huge cherry-tree grew outside, so close that its boughs
tapped against the house, and it was so thick-set with
blossoms that hardly a leaf was to be seen. On both sides
of the house was a big orchard, one of apple-trees and one
of cherry-trees, also showered over with blossoms; and their
grass was all sprinkled with dandelions. In the garden below
were lilac trees purple with flowers and their dizzily sweet
fragrance drifted up to the window on the morning wind.

Below the garden a green field lush with clover sloped
down to the hollow where the brook ran and where scores of

white birches grew, upspringing airily out of an undergrowth suggestive of delightful possibilities in ferns and mosses and woodsy things generally. Beyond it was a hill, green and feathery with spruce and fir; there was a gap in it where the gray gable end of the little house she had seen from the other side of the Lake of Shining Waters was visible.

Off to the left were the big barns and beyond the, away down over green, low-sloping fields, was a sparkling blue glimpse of the sea.

Anne's beauty-loving eyes lingered on it all, taking everything greedily in. She had looked on so many unlovely places in her life, poor child; but this was as lovely as anything she had ever dreamed.

*

Sir Walter Scott
Waverley (1814)

Filled almost with the expectation of beholding some 'old, old man, with beard as white as snow,' whom he might question concerning this deserted mansion, our hero turned to a little oaken wicket-door, well clenched with iron nails, which opened in the courtyard wall at its angle with the house. It was only latched, notwithstanding its fortified appearance, and, when opened, admitted him into the garden, which presented a pleasant scene. The southern side of the house, clothed with fruit-trees, and having many evergreens trained upon its walls, extended its irregular yet venerable front along a terrace, partly paved, partly gravelled, partly bordered with flowers and choice shrubs. This elevation descended by three several flights of steps, placed in its centre and at the extremities, into what might be called the garden proper, and was fenced along the top by a stone parapet with a heavy balustrade, ornamented from space to space with huge grotesque figures of animals seated upon their haunches, among which the favourite bear was repeatedly introduced. Placed in the middle of the terrace, between a sashed door opening from the house and the central flight of steps, a huge animal of the same species supported on his head and fore-paws a sundial of large circumference, inscribed with more diagrams than Edward's mathematics enabled him to decipher.

The garden, which seemed to be kept with great accuracy, abounded in fruit-trees, and exhibited a profusion of flowers and evergreens, cut into grotesque forms. It was laid out in terraces, which descended rank by rank from the western wall to a large brook, which had a tranquil and smooth appearance, where it served as a boundary to the garden; but, near the extremity, leapt in tumult over a strong dam, or weir-head, the cause of its temporary tranquillity, and there forming a cascade, was overlooked by an octagonal summer-house, with a gilded bear on the top by way of a vane. After this feat, the brook, assuming its natural rapid and fierce character, escaped from the eye down a deep and wooded dell, from the copse of which arose a massive, but ruinous tower, the former habitation of the Barons of Bradwardine. The margin of the brook, opposite to the garden, displayed a narrow meadow, or haugh, as it was called, which formed a small washing-green; the bank, which retired behind it, was covered by ancient trees.

*

William Dean Howells
Indian Summer (1886)

When he entered the beautiful old garden, its benison of
peace fell upon his tumult, and he began to breathe a freer
air, reverting to his purpose to be gone in the morning and
resting in it, as he strolled up the broad curve of its alley
from the gate. He had not been there since he walked there
with one now more like a ghost to him than any of the dead
who had since died. It was there that she had refused him; he
recalled with a grim smile the awkwardness of getting back
with her to the gate from the point, far within the garden,
where he had spoken. Except that this had happened in the
fall, and now it was early spring, there seemed no change
since then; the long years that had elapsed were like a
winter between.

He met people in groups and singly loitering through the
paths, and chiefly speaking English; but no one spoke to him,
and no one invaded the solitude in which he walked. But the
garden itself seemed to know him, and to give him a tacit
recognition; the great, foolish grotto before the gate, with its
statues by Bandinelli, and the fantastic effects of drapery and
flesh in party-coloured statues lifted high on either side of
the avenue; the vast shoulder of wall, covered thick with ivy
and myrtle, which he passed on his way to the amphitheatre
behind the palace; the alternate figures and urns on their
pedestals in the hemicycle, as if the urns were placed there
to receive the ashes of the figures when they became extinct;
the white statues or the colossal busts set at the ends of the
long, alleys against black curtains of foliage; the big fountain,
with its group in the centre of the little lake, and the meadow,

quiet and sad, that stretched away on one side from this; the keen light under the levels of the dense pines and ilexes; the paths striking straight on either hand from the avenue through which he sauntered, and the walk that coiled itself through the depths of the plantations; all knew him, and from them and from the winter neglect which was upon the place distilled a subtle influence, a charm, an appeal belonging to that combination of artifice and nature which is perfect only in an Italian garden under an Italian sky. He was right in the name which he mockingly gave the effect before he felt it; it was a debauch, delicate, refined, of unserious pensiveness, a smiling melancholy, in which he walked emancipated from his harassing hopes, and keeping only his shadowy regrets.

Colville did not care to scale the easy height from which you have the magnificent view, conscious of many photographs, of Florence. He wandered about the skirts of that silent meadow, and seeing himself unseen, he invaded its borders far enough to pluck one of those large scarlet anemones, such as he had given his gentle enemy. It was tilting there in the breeze above the unkempt grass, and the grass was beginning to feel the spring, and to stir and stretch itself after its winter sleep; it was sprinkled with violets, but these he did not molest. He came back to a stained and mossy stone bench on the avenue, fronting a pair of rustic youths carved in stone, who had not yet finished some game in which he remembered seeing them engaged when he was there before. He had not walked fast, but he had walked far, and was warm enough to like the whiffs of soft wind on his uncovered head. The spring was coming; that was its breath, which you know unmistakably in Italy after all the kisses that winter gives. Some birds were singing in the trees; down an alley into which he could look, between the high walls of green, he could see two people in flirtation: he waited patiently till the young man should put his arm round the girl's waist, for the fleeting embrace from which she pushed it and fled further down the path.

"Yes, it's spring," thought Colville; and then, with the selfishness of the troubled soul, he wished that it might be winter still and indefinitely.

＊

Edith Wharton
The Valley of Decision (1902)

The sense of strangeness inspired by his odd companion soon gave way in Odo's mind to emotions of delight and wonder. He was, even at that age, unusually sensitive to external impressions, and when the hunchback, after ascending many stairs and winding through endless back-passages, at length led him out on a terrace above the garden, the beauty of the sight swelled his little heart to bursting.

A Duke of Pianura had, some hundred years earlier, caused a great wing to be added to his palace by the eminent architect Carlo Borromini, and this accomplished designer had at the same time replanted and enlarged the ducal gardens. To Odo, who had never seen plantations more artful than the vineyards and mulberry orchards about Pontesordo, these perspectives of clipped beech and yew, these knots of box filled in with multi-coloured sand, appeared, with the fountains, colonnades and trellised arbours surmounted by globes of glass, to represent the very pattern and Paradise of gardens. It seemed indeed too beautiful to be real, and he trembled, as he sometimes did at the music of the Easter mass, when the hunchback, laughing at his amazement, led him down the terrace steps.

It was Odo's lot in after years to walk the alleys of many a splendid garden, and to pace, often wearily enough, the paths along which he was now led; but never after did he renew the first enchanted impression of the mystery and brightness that remained with him as the most vivid emotion of his childhood.

Though it was February the season was so soft that the orange and lemon trees had been put out in their earthen vases before the lemon-house, and the beds in the parterres were full of violets, daffodils and auriculas; but the scent of the orange-blossoms and the bright colours of the flowers moved Odo less than the noble ordonnance of the pleached alleys, each terminated by a statue or a marble seat; and when he came to the grotto where, amid rearing sea-horses and Tritons, a cascade poured from the grove above, his wonder passed into such delicious awe as hung him speechless on the hunchback's hand.

"Eh," said the latter with a sneer, "it's a finer garden than we have at our family palace. Do you know what's planted there?" he asked, turning suddenly on the little boy. "Dead bodies, cavaliere! Rows and rows of them; the bodies of my brothers and sisters, the Innocents who die like flies every year of the cholera and the measles and the purid fever." He saw the terror in Odo's face and added in a gentler tone: "Eh, don't cry, cavaliere; they sleep better in those beds than in any others they're like to lie on. Come, come, and I'll show your excellency the aviaries."

From the aviaries they passed to the Chinese pavilion,

where the Duke supped on summer evenings, and thence to the bowling-alley, the fish-stew and the fruit-garden. At every step some fresh surprise arrested Odo; but the terrible vision of that other garden planted with the dead bodies of the Innocents robbed the spectacle of its brightness, dulled the plumage of the birds behind their gilt wires and cast a deeper shade over the beech-grove, where figures of goat-faced men lurked balefully in the twilight. Odo was glad when they left the blackness of this grove for the open walks, where gardeners were working and he had the reassurance of the sky.

*

Marcel Proust

Remembrance of Things Past (1913–27)
Translated by C. K. Scott Moncrieff

It was the hour and season in which the Bois seems, perhaps, most multiform, not only because it is then most divided, but because it is divided in a different way. Even in the unwooded parts, where the horizon is large, here and there against the background of a dark and distant mass of trees, now leafless or still keeping their summer foliage unchanged, a double row of orange-red chestnuts seemed, as in a picture just begun, to be the only thing painted, so far, by an artist who had not yet laid any colour on the rest, and to be offering their cloister, in full daylight, for the casual exercise of the human figures that would be added to the picture later on.

Farther off, at a place where the trees were still all green, one alone, small, stunted, lopped, but stubborn in its resistance, was tossing in the breeze an ugly mane of red.

Elsewhere, again, might be seen the first awakening of this Maytime of the leaves, and those of an ampelopsis, a smiling miracle, like a red hawthorn flowering in winter, had that very morning all 'come out', so to speak, in blossom. And the Bois had the temporary, unfinished, artificial look of a nursery garden or a park in which, either for some botanic purpose or in preparation for a festival, there have been embedded among the trees of commoner growth, which have not yet been uprooted and transplanted elsewhere, a few rare specimens, with fantastic foliage, which seem to be clearing all round themselves an empty space, making room, giving air, diffusing light. Thus it was the time of year at which the Bois de Boulogne displays more separate characteristics, assembles more distinct elements in a composite whole than at any other. It was also the time of day. In places where the trees still kept their leaves, they seemed to have undergone an alteration of their substance from the point at which they were touched by the sun's light, still, at this hour in the morning, almost horizontal, as it would be a few hours later, at the moment when, just as dusk began, it would flame up like a lamp, project far over the leaves a warm and artificial glow, and set ablaze the few topmost boughs of a tree that would remain itself unchanged, a sombre incombustible candelabrum beneath its flaming crest. At one spot the light grew solid as a brick wall, and like a piece of yellow Persian masonry, patterned in blue, daubed coarsely upon the sky the leaves of the chestnuts; at another, it cut them off from the sky towards which they stretched out their curling, golden fingers. Half-way up the trunk of a tree draped with wild vine, the light had grafted and brought to blossom, too dazzling to be clearly distinguished, an enormous posy, of red flowers apparently, perhaps of a new variety of carnation. The different parts of the Bois, so easily confounded in summer in the density and monotony of their universal green, were now clearly divided. A patch of brightness indicated the approach to almost every one of them, or else a splendid mass of foliage stood out like an oriflamme. I could make out, as on a coloured map, Armenonville, the Pré Catalan, Madrid, the Race Course and the shore of the lake. Here and there would appear some meaningless erection, a sham grotto, a mill, for which the trees made room by drawing away from it, or which was borne upon the soft green platform of a grassy lawn. I could feel that the Bois was not really a wood, that it existed for a purpose alien to the life of its trees; my sense of exaltation was due not only to admiration of the autumn tints but to a bodily desire. Ample source of a joy which the heart feels at first without being conscious of its cause, without understanding that it results from no external impulse! Thus I gazed at the trees with an unsatisfied longing which went beyond them and, without my knowledge, directed itself towards that masterpiece of beautiful strolling women which the trees enframed for a few hours every day.

*

Robert Burton
The Anatomy of Melancholy (1621)

But the most pleasant of all outward pastimes is that of Aretaeus, *deambulatio per amoena loca*, to make a petty progress, a merry journey now and then with some good companions...to walk amongst orchards, gardens, bowers, mounts, and arbours, artificial wildernesses, green thickets, arches, groves. Lawns, rivulets, fountains, and such-like pleasant places, like that Antiochian Daphne, brooks, pools, fishponds, between wood and water, in a fair meadow, by a river-side, *ubi variae avium cantationes, florum colores, pratorum frutices,* etc., to disport in some pleasant plain, park, run up a steep hill sometimes, or sit in a shady seat, must needs be a delectable recreation. *Hortus principis et domus ad delectationem facta, cum sylva, monte et piscine, vulgo La Montagna:* the prince's garden at Ferrara Schottus highly magnifies, within the groves, mountains, ponds for a delectable prospect, he was much affected with it; a Persian paradise, or pleasure park, could not be more delectable in his sight. St. Bernard, in the description of his monastery, is almost ravished with the pleasures of it. 'A sick man,' (saith he) 'sits upon a green bank, and when the dog-star parcheth the plains and dries up rivers, he lies in a shady bower,' *Fronde sub arborea ferventia temperat astra,* 'and feeds his eye with variety of objects, herbs, trees, to comfort his misery, he receives many delightsome smells, and fills his ears with that sweet and various harmony of the birds. Good God' (saith he), 'what a company of pleasures hast Thou made for man!'

*

Henry James
The Awkward Age (1899)

The lower windows of the great white House, which stood high and square, opened to a wide flagged terrace, the parapet of which, an old balustrade of stone, was broken in the middle of its course by a flight of stone steps that descended to a wonderful garden. The terrace had the afternoon shade and fairly hung over the prospect that dropped away and circled it – the prospect, beyond the series of gardens, of scattered, splendid trees and green glades, an horizon mainly of woods. Nanda Brookenham, one day at the end of July, coming out to find the place unoccupied as yet by other visitors, stood there awhile with an air of happy possession. She moved from end to end of the terrace, pausing, gazing about her, taking in with a face that showed the pleasure of a brief independence the combination of delightful things—of old rooms with old decorations that gleamed and gloomed through the high windows, of old gardens that squared themselves in the wide angles of old walls, of wood-walks rustling in the afternoon breeze and stretching away to further reaches of solitude and summer. The scene had an expectant stillness that she was too charmed to desire to break; she watched it, listened to it, followed with her eyes the white butterflies among the flowers below her, then gave a start as the cry of a peacock came to her from an unseen alley. It set her after a minute into less difficult motion; she passed slowly down the steps, wandering further, looking back at the big bright house but pleased again to see no one else appear. If the sun was still high enough she had a pink parasol. She went through the gardens one by one, skirting the high walls that were so like 'collections' and thinking how, later on, the nectarines and plums would flush there. She expressed a friendly greeting with a man at work, passed through an open door and, turning this way and that, finally found herself in the park, at some distance from the house. It was a point she had to take another rise to reach, a place marked by an old green bench for a larger sweep of the view, which, in the distance, where the woods stopped, showed, in the most English way in the world, the colour-spot of an old red village and the tower of an old grey church. She had sunk down upon the bench almost with a sense of adventure, yet not too fluttered to wonder if it wouldn't have been happy to bring a book; the charm of which precisely would have been in feeling everything about her too beautiful to let her read.

*

Percy Lubbock
Earlham (1922)

It was superb, the great lawn at Earlham—it really was. I have described how it was lifted up, almost to the level, I should think, of the first floor windows, by a steep bank of shaven grass; but there was a considerable expanse on the lower level too, before you reached the bank. On this lower lawn, to right and left, there was a fantastic medley of flower-beds, cut in queer shapes, coils and lozenges and loops; and the gardener's fancy ran strangely riot, year by year, in selecting and disposing the flowers that filled them. Geraniums roasting-red, French marigolds orange and mahogany-coloured, the tomato-note of waxen begonias, exotic herbage all speckled and pied and ring-straked, dahlias, calceolarias—they were marshalled and massed together, they fought it out as they would. But indeed they were mastered by the sunshine, by the blaze of light in which they flashed and twinkled; and they fell back, right and left, leaving a wide space of clear clean grass unbroken. And then there rose before you the green bank, so steep that I wonder how the mowing-machine contrived to sidle along it and keep it thus smoothly shaven...

Wait however, wait and look nearer at the flower-beds, which lie in a rambling cluster, you remember, under the lip of the steep bank of grass. Their coiling serpentine forms are all confused in the darkness, but I can easily thread the narrow grassy paths that separate each from each. The bright colours of the geraniums and the salvias are veiled by night; the brightest red and blue, even the flaring orange of the marigolds, are softened and obscured so that you hardly notice them among the deep grey of the tufts and bushes. But wait—the scent of the night-flower leads me on, where the narrow way between the beds goes turning and twisting. And there—where this morning you saw nothing but tall stalks, broad leaves, drooping and discoloured flower-trumpets, look now! Pure and cool and snow-white the clear stars have opened with the fall of the dusk, and whiter and whiter they grow as the night deepens. This is the flower which sends that wave of fragrance into the stillness, the flower that shines in the garden at Earlham from dusk to dawn. Far into the August night, till the first quiver of day-break stirs the hush of the darkness, the white stars hang motionless on their tall stalks, facing to the sky. With the daylight they droop and fall; but in August the morning already delays, there are long hours after midnight before the polar clouds begin to catch the advancing light. Till then the night-flower blooms in its white splendour, awake and alone.

*

Giovanni Boccaccio

The Decameron (1358)

Whereupon they hied them to a walled garden adjoining the palace; which, the gates being opened, they entered, and wonder-struck by the beauty of the whole passed on to examine more attentively the several parts. It was bordered and traversed in many parts by alleys, each very wide and straight as an arrow and roofed in with trellis of vines, which gave good promise of bearing clusters that year, and being all in flower, dispersed such fragrance throughout the garden as blended with that exhaled by many another plant that grew therein made the garden seem redolent of all the spices that ever grew in the East. The sides of the alleys were all, as it were, walled in with roses white and red and jasmine; insomuch as there no part of the garden but what one might walk there not merely in the morning but at high noon in grateful shade and fragrance, completely screened from the sun. As for the plants that were in the garden, 'twere long to enumerate them, to specify their sorts, to describe the order of their arrangement; enough, in brief, that there was an abundance of every rarer species that our climate allows. In the middle of the garden, a thing not less but much more to be commended than aught else, was a lawn of the finest turf, so green that it seemed almost black, pranked with flowers of, perhaps, a thousand sorts , and girt about with the richest living verdure of orange-trees and cedars, which shewed and only flowers but fruits both new and old, and were no less grateful to the smell by their fragrance than to the eye by their shade. In the middle of the lawn was a basin of whitest marble, graven with marvellous art; in the centre whereof—

whether the spring were natural or artificial I know not—rose a column supporting a figure which sent forth a jet of water of such volume and to such an altitude that it fell, not without a delicious plash, into the basin in quantity amply sufficient to turn a mill wheel. The overflow was carried away from the lawn by a hidden conduit, and then, reemerging, was distributed through tiny channels, very fair and cunningly contrived, in such sort as to flow round the entire lawn, and by similar derivative channels to penetrate almost every part of the fair garden, until, re-uniting at a certain point, it issued thence, and, clear as crystal, slid down towards the plain, turning by the way two mill-wheels with extreme velocity, to the no small profit of the lord. The aspect of this garden, its fair order, the plants and the fountain and the rivulets that flowed from it, so charmed the ladies and the three young men that with one accord they affirmed that they not how it could receive any accession of beauty, or what other form could be given to Paradise, if it were to be planted on earth.

*

Walter de la Mare
"The Sunken Garden" from *The Sunken Garden* (1917)

Speak not,—whisper not;
Here bloweth thyme and bergamot;
Softly on the evening hour,
Secret herbs their spices shower,
Dark-spiked rosemary and myrrh,
Lean-stalked purple lavender;
Hides within her bosom, too,
All her sorrows, bitter rue.

Breathe not—trespass not;
Of this green and darkling spot,
Latticed from the moon's beams,
Perchance, a distant dreamer dreams;
Perchance upon its darkening air,
The unseen ghosts of children fare,
Faintly swinging, sway and sweep,
Like lovely sea-flowers in its deep;
While, unmoved, to watch and ward,
'Mid its gloom'd and daisied sward,
Stands with bowed and dewy head
That one little leaden Lad.

GARDEN MAKING

Given that most writers are not gardeners, it is remarkable how many of them are interested in the creation of gardens. This may be because garden design—especially when not followed through with all the attendant digging, planting, weeding and other dirty work—is a wonderful intellectual activity. Johan Wolfgang von Goethe, in *Elective Affinities*, constructed a whole novel around the design of a huge park, although the book is really about the psychological relationships of a couple and their friends at the heart of it. Similarly, much of Tom Stoppard's play *Arcadia* has to do with satirizing Humphry Repton, the great late Georgian landscape architect, and the coming fad for the picturesque gardening style. Thomas Love Peacock chose the same target in *Headlong Hall*, scoring a direct and very funny hit. More typically, James Boswell simply speculates on the sort of fine walled garden he would like to have, before being squashed by the thunderous opinions of Dr. Johnson, neither man being in fact any sort of expert. Robert Louis Stevenson, no less an amateur, creates (in theory) the ideal house—"inside the garden, we can construct a country of our own".

Yet there are true gardener-writers. The Czech playwright and journalist Karel Čapek is one, and his horticultural advice is irresistible, practical or otherwise. The seventeenth century Dutch poet-composer Constantijn Huygens not only designed a splendid estate and garden near the Hague but also wrote a long poem about it, and like Alexander Pope delighted in praising his own work. Pope, famously, had strong opinions on other people's failings in garden design (and expressed them), while the tenth century Chinese poet Su Shi settled for quietly planting dates, chestnuts and mulberries in his mountainside garden. Garden-makers one and all, in reality or imagination.

Karel Čapek

The Gardener's Year (1929)

There are a number of ways of laying out a garden. The best is by taking on a gardener. A gardener will set up all sorts of sticks, twigs and brooms for you which he will insist are Maples, Hawthorns, Elders, standards, half-standards and other natural species. Then he will root about in the earth, turn it over and tamp it down again, make little paths out of rubble, stick some sort of withered leaves in the ground here and there which he will call English Ryegrass and Brown Bent, Foxtail Grass, Dogstail and Cat Tail Grass, and afterwards he will depart, leaving behind him a garden which is brown and bare, as it was on the first day of the creation of the world; but he will impress upon you that you will need to water all this soil of the earth carefully every day and that when the grass comes out you will need to have some gravel delivered for the paths. Well, fine....

If you [water] every day, after a fortnight weeds will start to spring up instead of grass. It is one of the mysteries of nature why the most rampant, bristly weeds grow from the best grass seed. Perhaps weed seed should be sown in order for a nice lawn to sprout. After three weeks the lawn is densely overgrown with thistles and other wickednesses, creeping or rooted several feet into the ground. If you try to uproot them, they break off at the root or take whole clods of earth with them. It is like this: the greater the nuisance, the more it thrives....

Still, weeds have to be rooted out the lawn. You weed and weed and behind your steps the future lawn turns into bare, brown earth, as it was on the first day of the creation of the world. Only in two or three places does something like greenish mould break out, something merely suggested, scant, and like down. There is no doubt that it is grass. You tiptoe round it and drive away the sparrows; and while you are gaping at the earth, before you can say 'Jack Robinson', the first small leaves break out the Gooseberry bushes and Currant bushes. You will never catch sight of the spring.

Your attitude towards things has changed. If it rains, you say that it is raining on the garden. If the sun shines, it is not just shining any old how but shining on the garden. If it is night-time, you are pleased that the garden is resting.

One day, you will open your eyes and the garden will be green tall grass will be glistening with dew, and swollen, crimson buds will be looking out from a thicket of Rose crowns; and the trees will have aged and will be full and dark with heavy tops and full, decayed scents in the damp shade. And you will not remember the frail, bare, brown garden of those days anymore, the uncertain down of the first grass, the meagre flowering of the first buds or all this clayey, poor, touching beauty of the garden as it has been laid out.

*

Robert Louis Stevenson
"The Ideal House" from *Essays of Travel* (1905)

Given these two prime luxuries, the nature of the country we are to live in is, I had almost said, indifferent; after that inside the garden we can construct a country of our own. Several old trees, a considerable variety of level, well-grown hedges to divide our garden into provinces, a good extent of old well-set turf, and thickets of shrubs and ever-greens to be cut into and cleared at the new owner's pleasure, are the qualities to be sought for in your promised land. Nothing is more delightful than a succession of small lawns, opening one out of the other through tall hedges; these have all the charm of the old bowling-green repeated, do not require the labour of many trimmers, and afford a series of changes. You must have much lawn against the early summer, so as to have a great field of daisies, the year's morning frost; as you must have a wood of lilacs, to enjoy to the full the period of their blossoming. Hawthorn is another of the spring's ingredients; but it best to have a rough public lane at one side of your enclosure which, at the right season, shall become an avenue of bloom and odour. The old flowers are the best and should grow carelessly in corners. Indeed, the ideal fortune is to find an old garden, once very richly cared for, since sunk into neglect, and to tend, not repair, that neglect. It will thus have a smack of nature and wildness which skilful dispositions cannot overtake. The gardener should be an idler, and have gross partiality to the kitchen plots: an eager or toilful gardener misbecomes the garden landscape; a tasteful gardener will be ever meddling, will keep the borders raw, and take the bloom off nature. Close adjoining, if you are in the south, an olive-yard, if in the north a swarded apple-orchard reaching to the stream, completes your miniature domain; but this perhaps best entered through a door in the high fruit-wall; so that you close the door behind you on your sunny plots, your hedges and ever-green jungle, when you go down to watch the apples falling in the pool. It is a golden maxim to cultivate the garden for the nose, and the eyes will take care of themselves. Nor must the ear be forgotten: without birds a garden is a prison-yard. There is a garden near Marseilles on a steep hill-side, walking by which, upon a sunny morning, your ear will suddenly be ravished with a burst of small and very cheerful singing; but the price paid, to keep so many ardent and winged creatures from their liberty, will make the luxury too dear for any thoughtful pleasure-lover. There is only one sort of bird that I can tolerate caged, though even then I think it hard, and that is what is called in France the Bec-d'Argent. I once had two of these pigmies in captivity; and in the quiet, hire house upon a silent street where I was then living, their song, which was not much louder than a bee's, but airily musical, kept me in a perpetual good humour. I put the cage upon my table when I worked, carried it with me when I went for meals, and kept it by my head at night: the first thing in the morning, these *maestrini* would pipe up. But these, even if you can pardon their imprisonment, are for the house. In the garden the wild birds must plant a colony, the chorus of the lesser warblers that should be almost deafening, a blackbird in the lilacs, a nightingale down the lane, so that you must stroll to hear it, and yet a little farther, tree-tops populous with rooks.

*

Thomas Love Peacock
Headlong Hall (1816)

'I perceive,' said Mr. Milestone, after they had walked a few paces, 'these grounds have never been touched by the finger of taste.'

'The place is quite a wilderness,' said Squire Headlong:

'for, during the latter part of my father's life, while I was finishing my education, he troubled himself about nothing but the cellar, and suffered everything else to go to rack and ruin. A mere wilderness, as you see, even now in December; but in the summer a complete nursery of briers, a forest of thistles, a plantation of nettles, without any live-stock but goats, that have eaten up all the bark of the trees. Here you see in the pedestal of a statue, with only half a leg and four toes remaining: there were many here once. When I was a boy, I used to sit every day on the shoulders of Hercules: what became of him I have never been able to ascertain. Neptune has been lying these seven years in the dust-hole; Atlas had his head knocked off to fit him for propping a shed; and only the day before yesterday we fished Bacchus out of the horse-pond.'

'My dear sir,' said Mr. Milestone, 'accord me your permission to wave the wand of enchantment over your grounds. The rocks shall be blown up, the trees shall be cut down, the wilderness and all its goats shall vanish like mist. Pagodas and Chinese bridges, gravel walks and shrubberies, bowling-greens, canals, and clumps of larch, shall rise upon its ruins. One age, sir, has brought to light the treasures of ancient learning; a second has penetrated into the depths of metaphysics; a third has brought to perfection the science of astronomy; but it was reserved for the exclusive genius of the present times, to invent the noble art of picturesque gardening, which has given, as it were, a new tint to the complexion of nature, and a new outline to the physiognomy of the universe!'

*

Tom Stoppard
Arcadia (1992)

Lady Croom Your drawing is a very wonderful transformation. I would not have recognized my own garden but for your ingenious book—is it not?—look! Here is the Park as it appears to us now, and here it is as it might be when Mr Noakes is done with it. Where there is the familiar pastoral refinement of an Englishman's garden, here is an eruption of gloomy forest and towering crag, of ruins where there never was a house, of water dashing against rocks where there was neither spring nor a stone I could throw the length of a cricket pitch. My hyacinth dell is become a haunt for hobgoblins, my Chinese bridge, which I am assured is superior to the one Kew, and for all I know at Peking, is usurped by a fallen obelisk overgrown with briars—

Noakes (*bleating*) Lord Little has one very similar—

Lady Croom I cannot relieve Lord Little's misfortunes by adding to my own. Pray, what is this rustic hovel that presumes to superimpose itself on my gazebo?

Noakes That is the hermitage, madam.

Lady Croom I am bewildered.

Brice It is all very irregular, Mr Noakes.

Noakes It is, sir. Irregularity is one of the chiefest principles of the picturesque style.

Lady Croom But Sidley Park is already a picture, and a most amiable picture too. The slopes are green and gentle. The trees are companionably grouped at intervals that show them to advantage. The rill is a serpentine ribbon unwound from the lake peaceably contained by meadows on which the right amount of sheep are tastefully arranged—in short, it is nature as God intended, and I can say with the painter , 'Et in Arcadia ego!' 'Here I am in Arcadia,' Thomasina.

Thomasina Yes, mama, if you would have it so.

Lady Croom Is she correcting my taste or my translation?

Thomasina Neither are beyond correction, but it was your geography that caused the doubt.

*

Louisa May Alcott
Little Women (1868)

The garden had to be put in order, and each sister had a quarter of the little plot to do what she liked with. Hannah used to say, 'I'd know which each of them gardings belonged to, ef I see 'em in Chiny,' and so she might, for the girls's tastes differed as much as their characters. Meg had roses and heliotrope, myrtle and a little orange tree in it. Jo's bed was never alike two seasons, for she was always trying experiments. This year it was to be a plantation of sunflowers, the seeds of which cheerful and aspiring plant were to feed Aunt Cockle-top and her family of chicks. Beth had old-fashioned, fragrant flowers in her garden—sweet peas and mignonette, larkspur, pinks, pansies, and southern-wood, with chickweed for the birds and catnip for the pussies. Amy had a bower in hers, rather small and earwiggy, but very pretty to look at, with honeysuckles and morning glories hanging their coloured horns and bells in graceful wreaths all over it; tall white lilies, delicate ferns and as many brilliant, picturesque plants as would consent to blossom there.

*

Horace Walpole
Letter to George Montagu, November 8, 1755

My Dear Sir

You oblige me extremely by giving me this commission; and though I am exceedingly unlike Solomon in everything else, I will at least resemble him in remembering you to the Hiram, from whom I obtained my cedars of Lebanon. He is by men called Christopher Gray, nurseryman at Fulham. I mention cedars first, because they are the most beautiful of the evergreen race, and because they are the dearest; half a guinea a-piece in baskets. The arbutus are scarce a crown a-piece, but they are very beautiful; the lignum-vitae I would not recommend to you; they stink abominably if you touch them, and never make a handsome tree; the Chinese arbor-vitae is very beautiful. I have a small nursery myself, scarce bigger than one of those pleasant gardens which Solomon describes, and which if his fair one meant the church, I suppose must have meant the church-yard. Well, out of this little parsley-bed of mine, I can furnish you with a few plants, particularly

three Chinese arbor-vitaes, a dozen of the New England or
lord Weymouth's pine, which is that beautiful tree, that we
have so much admired at the duke of Argyle's for its clean,
straight stem, the lightness of its hairy green, and for being
feathered quite to the ground; they should stand in moist soil,
and care must be taken every year to clear away all plants
and trees round them, that they may have free air and room
to expand themselves. Besides these I shall send you twelve
stone or italian pines, twelve pineasters, twelve black spruce
firs, two Caroline cherries, thirty evergreen cytisus, a pretty
shrub that grows very fast, and may be cut down as you
please; fifty Spanish brooms, and six acacias, the genteelest
tree of all, but you must take care to plant them in a first
row, and where they will be well sheltered, for the least wind
tears and breaks them to pieces. All these are ready, whenever
you will give me directions, how, and where to send them.
They are exceedingly small, as I have but lately taken to
propagate myself; but then they will travel more safely, will
be more sure of living, and will grow faster than larger. Other
sorts of evergreens that you must have, are silver and scotch
firs; Virginia cedars, which should stand forward and have
nothing touch them; and above all cypresses, which, I think,
are my chief passion; there is nothing so picturesque, where
they stand two or three in a clump, upon a little hillock, or
rising above low shrubs, and particularly near buildings.
There is another bit of picture, or which I am fond, and that
is a larch or a spruce fir planted behind a weeping willow, and
shooting upwards as the willow depends. I think for courts
about a house, or winter gardens, almond trees mixed with
evergreens, particularly with scotch firs, have a pretty effect,
before anything else comes out; whereas almond trees, being

generally planted among other trees, and being in bloom before other trees have leaves, have no ground to shew the beauty of their blossoms. Gray at Fulham sells cypresses in pots at half a crown a-piece; you turn them out of the pot with all their mould, and they never fail. I think this is all you mean; if you have any more garden- questions or commissions, you know you command my little knowledge.

*

Gervase Markham
Country Farm (1616)

The Garden of Pleasure shall be set about and compassed with arbors made of jessamin, rosemarie, box, juniper, cypress-trees, savin, cedars, rose-trees and other dainties first planted and pruned according as the nature of every one doth require, but after brought into some form and order with willow or juniper poles, such as may serve for the making of arbors. The ways and alleys must be covered and sown with fine sand well beat, or with the powder of the sawing of marble, or else paved handsomely with good pit stone.

This garden, by means of a large path of the breadth of six feet, shall be divided into two equal parts; the one shall contain the herbs and flowers used to make nosegays and garlands of, as March violets, Provence gillyflowers, purple gillyflowers, Indian gillyflowers, small pansies, daisies, yellow and white gillyflowers, marigolds, lily connally, daffodils, Canterbuiry bells, purple velvet flowers, anemones, corn-flag, mugwort, lilies and other such-like; and it may be indeed the Nosegay Garden.

The other part shall have all other sweet-smelling herbs whether they be such as bear no flowers, or, if they bear any, yet they are not oput in nosegays alone, but the whole herb be with them, as Southernwood, wormwood, pellitory, rosemary, jessamine, marierom, balm-mints, pennyroyal, costmarie, hyssop, lavender, basil, sage, savory, rue, tansy, thyme, camomile, mugwort, bastard marierum, nept, sweet balm, all-good, anis, horehound and other such-like; and this mmay be called the garden for herbs and good smell.

These sweet herbs and flowers for nosegays shall be set in order upon beds and quarters of such-like length and breadth as those in the kitchen garden; others in mazes made for the pleasing and recreating of the sight, and other some are set in proportions made of beds interlaced and drawn one within another or broken off with borders, or without borders.

*

John Galsworthy
The Country House (1907)

At one end of the walled garden which Mr Pendyce had formed in imitation of that at dear old Strathbegally, was a virgin orchard of pear and cherry trees. They blossomed early, and by the end of the third week or April the last of the cherries had broken into flower. In the long grass, underneath, a wealth of daffodils, jonquils, and narcissus, came up year after year, and sunned their yellow stars in the light which dappled though the blossom.

And here Mrs Pendyce would come, tan gauntlets on her hands, and stand, her face a little flushed with stooping, as though the sight of all that bloom was restful. It was due to her that these old trees escaped year after year the pruning and improvements which the genius of the Squire would otherwise have applied. She had been brought up in an old Totteridge tradition that fruit-trees should be left to themselves, while her husband, possessed of a grasp of the subject not more than usually behind the times, was all for newer methods. She had fought for those trees. They were as yet the only things she had fought for in her married life, and Horace Pendyce still remembered with a discomfort robbed by time of poignancy how she stood with her back to their bedroom door and said, "If you cut those poor trees, Horace, I won't live here!" He had at once expressed his determination to have them pruned; but having put off the action for a day or two, the trees still stood unpruned thirty-three years later. He had even come to feel rather proud of the fact that they continued to bear fruit, and would speak of them thus: "Queer fancy of my wife's, never been cut. And yet, remarkable thing, they do better than any of the others!"

*

John Hollander
"Instructions to the Landscaper" from *Harp Lake* (1988)

V. If there are to be ornamental gates representing Virtues, paths of ancient Rightness, temples to the spirits of time and place, then let each one, half-hidden from many viewpoints in the luxuriance of green, afford a prospect of one of the others: from one side of the rounded Temple of Honor, for example, it is appropriate that one should see, perfectly framed by two of the fluted columns, huddling in the rocks by the long water, the Grotto of Fear.

—

VII. If the Garden has been properly laid out, there need not be a maze in it. For the quest, the puzzlement, the contingency of a place of rest with its bench and rosebushes in the center of it all, the ease of entrance and its welcoming entrapment, the problems of homing, will all have been provided by the Garden itself. And the maze's parable, unrolling beneath the hurrying feet of the last wanderers on a summer evening that now chills and darkens—the parable of how there can be no clarity of truth without puzzlement, no joy without losing one's way—will be propounded by the Garden's final perfection, namely, that in it is no trace of the designer, that no image of him can ever be found. He—you—will have disappeared into the ground of the place that has been made.

*

Osbert Sitwell
Penny Foolish (1936)

Flowers, I have written, should be confined to a flower-garden; but, even there, they should form only the borders to long, rolling waves of sea-green cabbages and be interspersed with the purple pom-poms of the artichoke, with the knobs of onions and the scarlet flowers of the bean.

Moreover, the few flowers you have, should be very

specially chosen, selected for their beauty in dying and in death as much for their beauty in the full unfolding of life; that is to say, one should be as much influenced by their habits of growth as by their blossom. For what is life, except a long process—varying individually, it is true, in its length—of death? And just as the Greeks used to maintain that no man could be happy or fortunate until he was dead, so can no flower be considered beautiful until it is fallen. Thus the Chinese, most wise and subtle race, allow the quality of beauty to no flower which does not maintain an exquisite form and colour even in its decay. So it will be seen that a fruit tree is more beautiful than, for example, a sweet pea; for in the spring it is a little fragrant cloud anchored to the ground, in summer its branches are heavy with shapes carved of true jade, and in the autumn weighted down with tinted and pleasant fruit. How dismal, as opposed to this excellence, enduring all the year, are the brown, tattered remnants of Michaelmas daisy and chrysanthemum!

.   *

Colette
"The Advice" (1924) from *The Collected Stories of Colette*
Edited by Robert Phelps

Old Monsieur Mestre again poured one can of water on the bleeding hearts, one on the newly-planted heliotropes, and two on the blue hydrangeas, which were always dying of the thirst. He tied up the nasturtiums, eager to climb, and with the shears he clipped the last withered thyrsus of the lilacs with a little cry, 'Ha!' and wiped the dirt from his hands. His little garden in Auteuil, densely planted, well watered, and neatly arranged like a too-small parlour, was overflowing with flowers and defying the dryness of June. Up until November it astonished the eyes—those of the passers-by at least—for Monsieur Mestre, stooped over his walled rectangle of earth for hours, tended it from morning to night, with the doggedness of a truck farmer. He planted, grafted and pruned; he hunted down slugs, small suspicious-looking spiders, the green flies, and the blight bug. When night came, he would clap his hands together, exclaim 'Ha!' and instead of dreaming over the phlox, haunted by grey sphinx moths beneath the white wisteria entwined with purple wisteria, and spurning the fiery geraniums, he would turn away from his charming handiwork and go off for a smoke in his kitchen, or stroll along the boulevards of Auteuil.

The lovely May evening had prolonged his day as amateur gardener by an hour after dinner. The sky, the pale gravel path, the white flowers, and the white façades held a light which did not want to end, and mothers, standing the doorways of the little open houses, called in vain to their children, who preferred the dusty warm sidewalk to their cool beds.

*

John Parkinson
Paradisi in Sole Paradisus Terrestris (1629)

Your knots or beds being prepared fitly,...you may place or order your roots therein thus; Either many roots of one kind set together in a round or cluster, or long wayes crosse a bed one by another, whereby the beauty of many flowers of one kinde being together, may make a fair show well pleasing to many: or else you may plant one or two in a place dispersedly over the whole knot, or in a proportion or diameter one place answering another of the knot, as your store will suffer you or your knot permit: Or you may also mingle those roots in their planting, many of divers sorts together, that they may give the more glorious shew when they are in flower; and that you may do so, you may first observe the several kindes of them, which do flower at one and the same time, and then to place them in such order and so near to one another, that their flowers appearing together of several colours, will cause the more admiration in the beholders.

*

Laurence Sterne
Tristram Shandy (Vol 6, 1762)

If the reader has not a clear conception of the rood and a half of ground which lay at the bottom of my uncle *Toby*'s kitchen garden, and which was the scene of so many of his delicious hours,—the fault is not in me,—but in his imagination;—for I am sure I gave him so minute a description, I was almost ashamed of it.

When FATE was looking forwards one afternoon, into the great transactions of future times,—and recollected for what purposes, this little plot, by a decree fast bound down in iron, had been destined,—she gave a nod to NATURE— 'twas enough—Nature threw half a spade full of her kindliest compost upon it, with just so *much* clay in it, as to retain the forms of angles and indentings,--and so *little* or it too, as not to cling to the spade, and render works of so much glory, nasty in foul weather.

My uncle *Toby* came down, as the reader has been informed, with plans along with him, of almost every fortified town in *Italy* and *Flanders;* so let the Duke of *Marlborough*, or the allies, have set down before what town they pleased, my uncle *Toby* was prepared for them.

His way, which was the simplest one in the world, was this: as soon as ever a town was invested—(but sooner when the design was known) to take a plan of it, (let it be what town it would) and enlarge it upon a scale to the exact size of his bowling green; upon the surface of which, by means of a large roll of packthread, and a number of small piquets driven into the ground, at the several angles and redans, he transferred the lines from his paper, then taking the profile of the place, with its works, to determine the depths and slopes of the ditches,—the talus of the glacis, and the precise height of the several banquets, parapets, &c.—he set the corporal to work—and sweetly it went on:—The nature of the soil,—the nature of the work itself,—and above all, the good nature of my uncle *Toby* sitting by from morning until night, chatting kindly with the corporal upon past-done deeds,—left LABOUR little else but the ceremony of the name.

*

James Shirley

"The Garden" from *Poems* (1646)

This garden does not take my eyes,
Though here you shew how art of men
Can purchase Nature at a price
Would stock old Paradise agen.

These glories while you dote upon,
I envie not your Spring nor pride,
Nay boast the Summer all your own,
My thoughts with lesse are satisfied.

Give me a little plot of ground,
Where I might with the Sun agree,
Though every day he walk the Round,
My garden he should seldom see.

Those Tulips that such wealth display,
To court my eye, shall lose their name,
Though now they listen, as if they
Expected I should praise their flame.

But I would see my self appear
Within the Violet's drooping head,
On which a melancholy tear
The discontented Morne hath shed.

Within their buds let Roses sleep,
And virgin Lillies on their stemme,
Till sighes from Lovers glide, and creep
Into their leaves to open them.
I' th' Center of my ground compose
Of Bayes and Ewe my Summer room,
Which may so oft as I repose,
Present my Arbour, and my Tombe.

No woman here shall find me out,
Or if a chance do bring one hither,
I'll be secure, for round about
I'll moat it with my eyes foul weather.

No Bird shall live within my pale,
To charme me with their shames of Art,
Unless some wandring Nightingale
Comes here to sing, and Break her heart.

Upon whose death I'll try to write
An Epitaph in some funeral stone,
So sad, and true, it may invite
My self to die, and prove mine owne.

*

Charles Dudley Warner

My Summer in a Garden (1870)

Let us celebrate the soil. Most men toil that they may own a piece of it; they measure their success in life by their ability to buy it. It is alike the passion of the *parvenu* and the pride of the aristocrat. Broad acres are a patent of nobility; and no man but what feels more of a man in the world if he have a bit of ground that he can call his own. However small it is on the surface, it is four thousand miles deep; and that is a very handsome property. And there is great pleasure in working the soil, apart from the ownership of it. The man who has planted a garden feels that he has done something for the good of the world. He belongs to the producers. It is a pleasure to eat of the fruit of one's toil, if it be nothing more than a head of lettuce or an ear of corn. One cultivates a lawn, even, with great satisfaction; for there is nothing more beautiful than grass and turf in our latitude. The tropics may have their delights; but they have not turf: and the world without turf in a dreary desert. The original Garden of Eden could not have had such turf as one sees in England. The Teutonic races all love turf; they emigrate in the line of its growth.

*

Alphonse Daudet

Fromont and Risler (1874)

'When I am rich,' the little man used to say in his cheerless rooms in the Marais, 'I will have a house of my own, at the gates of Paris, almost in the country, a little garden which I will plant and water myself. That will be better for my health than all the excitement of the capital.'

Well, he had his house now, but he did not enjoy himself in it. It was at Montrouge, on the road that runs around the city. 'A small chalet, with garden,' said the advertisement, printed on a placard which gave an almost exact idea of the dimensions of the property. The papers were new and of rustic design, the paint perfectly fresh; a water-butt planted beside a vine-clad arbor played the part of a pond. In addition to all these advantages, only a hedge separated this paradise from another 'chalet with garden' of precisely the same description, occupied by Sigismond Planus the cashier, and his sister. To Madame Chebe that was a most precious circumstance. When the good woman was bored, she would take a stock of knitting and darning and go and sit in the old maid's arbor, dazzling her with the tale of her past splendors. Unluckily, her husband had not the same source of distraction.

However, everything went well at first. It was midsummer, and M. Chebe, always in his shirt-sleeves, was busily employed in getting settled. Each nail to be driven in the house was the subject of leisurely reflections, of endless discussions. It was the same with the garden. He had determined at first to make an English garden of it, lawns always green, winding paths shaded by shrubbery. But the trouble of it was that it took so long for the shrubbery to grow.

'I have a mind to make an orchard of it,' said the impatient little man.

And thenceforth he dreamed of nothing but vegetables, long lines of beans, and peach-trees against the wall. He dug for whole mornings, knitting his brows in a preoccupied way and wiping his forehead ostentatiously before his wife, so that she would say:

'For heaven's sake, do rest a bit—you're killing yourself.'

The result was that the garden was a mixture: flowers and fruit, park and kitchen garden; and whenever he went into Paris M. Chebe was careful to decorate his buttonhole with a rose from his rose-bushes.

*

Constantin Huygens
Hofwijk (1596-1687)
Translated by Peter Davidson and Adriaan van der Weel

Where are we now? Between the wood and orchard. Stay a while,

This too is my estate, my wishes give it form.

What I have wished for here will not, I trust, be dull.

Here by my wish stand two walls of the white poplars

Which reach to heaven now and flaunt their crowns of branches

(In a century, remember!) as far as the North dunes,

Well may they flaunt in pride, well may they pride themselves

As marksmen who protect the trees and herbs and flowers;

And should these die, and should they withered fall,

While poplars stand on guard, old age alone's the cause...

Briefly, there's a mid-line which parts Hofwijk in two

To which the left and right are balanced perfectly:

An East gate and a West, West avenue and East,
An East island and West, with equal paths enclosed,
The orchard lies midway, a forecourt, moat and house,
The south side to the Vliet lies open for our pleasure.
Now, if this could be weighed like gold in balanced scales
The house would be the pivot, scales level either side.
Who carps at symmetries like this must hate himself,
His own shape which God made. Before spade touched
the soil,
I let the precepts of the wise guide my design.
Examining myself, I sought no model more.
Two windows, then, for sight, nostrils as well as ears,
Two shoulders either side, two hips where they belong,
A thigh to either side, a knee, a foot, a leg;
That shape is God's own work and it is therefore good,
Whichever way I looked, I failed to find a rule
That bettered this: I cried, *Away, oblique,*
Irregular, twisted things, disjunctions lacking rule...

*

Prince Charles-Joseph de Ligne
Coup d'Oeil at Beloeil (1795)
Translated by Basil Gray

What a delight to go from one of these dwellings to another,
through a dense wood that is shrouded in mystery, lighted by
love alone! My thickly set trees would then cast shadows on
a person's complexion, bloom...and reputation. Others, who
would not have to take such precautions (for, after a while,

everybody knows everything about everyone else, and let the chips fall where they may), would be led by aromatic plants, like honeysuckle, edging little paths that would prevent them from losing their way between pavilions. What a misfortune if such a mistake were to reveal the mysteries of another dwelling! Couples who love one another ought to have a place set apart especially for them. (It would undoubtedly be empty more often than not.) They would have a voluptuous and varied garden because that is what would amuse them most suitably. Those who know neither how to wed nor how to love will not often be seen in the midst of the company. Save for a few greening rooms that can be closed off, marked by a little hedge amid a few clumps of trees, in case curiosity seekers are found loitering in this delightful setting, all the rest would open, including the public promenade. [There will be] no specified hours struck by those strident bells that call monks to their refectory. Eat and go to bed when you please. Nor [will there be] obligatory games of chance, those stupefiers of conversation and sociable life. They would disturb the air of tranquillity that this countryside must exude. In different circumstances I would prefer them to others, perhaps, since tyhey do not last so long, and I would rather people waste their money than their time, for every minute is precious.

—

The greatest misfortune for garden designers is not to be able to have an overall plan before beginning to work. A plot of ground in the neighbourhood of the garden is put up for sale and is purchased. Additions are created, but badly. Arrangements are made that, more than anything, derange.

Buildings take precedence over plantings, and what plantings there are do not appear to advantage. An unvaried expanse is no place for establishing viewpoints, especially where the visitor can be observed from all sides. The owner thinks he has a garden; he has everything but that.

*

Su Shi (1037–1101)
From "Eight Poems on Eastern Slope" (1081)
Translated by Stephen Owen

Though these weed-filled fields have run wild,
there are crops that suit its high and low spots.

In the damp bottoms I will plant my rice,
set dates and chestnuts on flats to the east.

This scholar of Shu in the Southland
has already been offered mulberries.

And good bamboos are not hard to grow—
I just worry that the shoots will spread uncontrolled.

I still have to choose a fine spot
and measure it out to site my house.

When my servant boy burned the dry grass,
he ran to tell me a well was uncovered:

I don't yet dare expect full meals,
but of a bucket of water I am assured.

*

Alexander Pope
Epistle IV to the Right Honorable Richard, Earl of Burlington (1731)

To build, to plant, whatever you intend
To rear the column, or the arch to bend,
To swell the terrace, or to sink the grot,
In all let Nature never be forgot.
Bu treat the goddess like a modest fair:
Not overdress, nor leave her wholly bare.
Let not each beauty everywhere be spied,
When half the skill is decently to hide.
He gains all points who pleasingly confounds,
Surprises, varies, and conceals the bounds.
Consult the genius of the place in all:
That tells the waters or to rise or fall;
Or helps th'ambitious hill the heav'ns to scale,
Or scoops in circling theatres the vale;
Calls in the country, catches op'ning glades,
Joins willing woods, and varies shades from shades;
Now breaks and now directs th'intending lines;
Paints as you plant, and as you work, designs.

*

Johann Wolfgang von Goethe
Elective Affinities (1809)

'The first thing we ought to do,' said the Captain, 'would be for me to make a compass survey of the area. It is a simple and pleasant job, and if it doesn't ensure absolute accuracy it is always useful and makes a good beginning; moreover, you can do it without much assistance and you know you'll get through it. Should you later think of making a more exact survey it would always be possible to take advice on that.'

The captain was very experienced at this sort of surveying. He had brought with him the necessary instruments and started on it at once. He instructed Eduard and some of the local trappers and peasants who were to assist him. The days went very well. He spent the evenings and early mornings on his map, drawing the contours and hatching the heights. Soon everything was shaded and contoured and Eduard saw his possessions taking shape on the paper like a new creation. It seemed to him that only now was he coming to know them, only now did they really belong to him.

Occasions for discussing the neighbourhood and the grounds can be created much more readily after a review like this than if you are merely trying out individual chance ideas on the spot, he thought.

'We must make that clear to my wife,' said Eduard.

'No, don't do that!' replied the captain, who did not like crossing other people's opinions with his own. Experience had taught him that human opinion is much too various to be unanimous on so much as a single point even in regard to the most reasonable proposition. 'Don't do that!' he said.

'She could easily become confused. Like all who engage in such things only for amusement she is more concerned to do something that that something should be done. This sort of person fumbles with nature, prefers this little spot or that, dares not venture to remove this or that obstacle, isn't bold enough to sacrifice anything, cannot imagine in advance what is supposed to be created, experiments—it may work out, it may not—makes changes and changes perhaps what ought to be left alone, and so in the end remains nothing but a hotch-potch that may turn out to be pleasing and stimulating but can never fully satisfy.'

'Confess it honestly,' said Eduard, 'you don't like the way she has laid out the park, do you?'

*

Samuel Pepys
Diary (22 July 1666)

...Walked up and down with Hugh May, who is a very ingenious man—among other things, discoursing of the present fashion of gardens, to make them plain—that we have the best walks of Gravell in the world—France having none, nor Italy; and our green of our bowling- alleys is better than any they have. So our business here being ayre, this is the best way, only with a little mixture of Statues or pots, which may be handsome, and so filled with another pot of such or such, a flower or greene, as the season of the year will bear. And then for Flowers, they are best seen in a little plat by themselves; besides, their borders spoil any other garden. And then for fruit, the best way is to have Walls built Circularly, one within another, to the South, on purpose for fruit, and leave the walking-garden only for that use.

*

James Boswell
Life of Johnson (1791)

BOSWELL. 'I wish to have a good walled garden.' JOHNSON. 'I don't think it would be worth the expense to you. We compute, in England, a park wall at a thousand pounds a mile; now a garden wall much cost at least as much. You intend your trees should grow higher than a deer will leap. Now let us see; for a hundred pounds you could have only forty-four square yards, which is very little; for two hundred pounds you may have eighty-four square yards, which is very well. But when will you get the value of two hundred pounds of walls, in fruit, in your climate? No, Sir; such contention with nature is not worth while. I would plant an orchard, and have plenty of such fruit as ripen well in your country. My friend, Dr. Madden, of Ireland, said, that "In an orchard there should be enough to eat, enough to lay up, enough to be stolen, and enough to rot upon the ground." Cherries are an early fruit; you may have them; and you may have the early apples and pears.' BOSWELL. 'We cannot have nonpareils.' JOHNSON. Sir, you can no more have nonpareils than you can grapes.' BOSWELL. 'We have them, Sir; but they are very bad.' JOHNSON. 'Nay, Sir, never try to have a thing merely to show that you *cannot* have it. From ground that would let for forty shillings you may have a large orchard; and you see it costs you only forty shillings. Nay, you may graze the ground when the trees are grown up; you cannot while they are young.' BOSWELL. 'Is not a good garden a very common thing in England, Sir?' JOHNSON. 'Not so common, Sir, as you imagine. In Lincolnshire there is hardly an orchard; in Staffordshire, very little fruit.' BOSWELL. 'Has Langton no orchard?' JOHNSON. 'No, Sir.' BOSWELL. 'How so, Sir?' JOHNSON. 'Why, Sir, from the general negligence of the country. He has not, because nobody else has it.' BOSWELL. 'A hothouse is a certain thing; I may have that.' JOHNSON. 'A hothouse is pretty certain; but you must first build it, then you must keep fires in it, and you must have a gardener to take care of it.' Boswell. 'But if I have a gardener at any rate?' JOHNSON. 'Why, yes.' BOSWELL. 'I'd have it near my house; there is no need to have it in the orchard.' JOHNSON. 'Yes, I'd have it near my house. I would plant a great many currants; the fruit is good, and they make a pretty sweetmeat.'

ENTHUSIASM

Some gardens are simply too wonderful to be objective about them. This, at least, is the impression you get from reading the ecstatic descriptions by some writers of what they have seen, or grown. Enthusiastic to the point of speechlessness (not that many true writers are ever at a loss for words), such effusions demonstrate just how certain horticultural achievements—and not just the grandest or most expert—can touch off virtual explosions of praise. Of course the gardens themselves may indeed warrant it, even such specimens as Dr. Delany's minuscule Irish example. As Edward Lear says of his own 'roziz', 'O criky! It's a dream!'

It is difficult not to have sympathy here. Admiration

for natural beauty seems to be a human characteristic and as readers, we are prepared to go along. Sir Roy Strong's account of Cecil Beaton's garden makes it sound as delicious as it probably was. Alexander Pope recognizes that his pride in his grotto may be slightly over the top ('You'll think that I have been very poetical in this description') but is convincing anyway, while Emily Carr's simple statement that 'We did have good times in that old garden' says quite enough. The enthusiasm is never cold; what's always explicit, and memorable, is the pleasure.

Edward Lear
Postscript to a letter to Lord Carlingford, (30 April 1885)

And this is certain; if so be
You could just now my garden see,
The aspic of my flowers so bright
Would make you shudder with delight.

And if you voz to see my roziz
As is a boon to all men's noziz,—
You'd fall upon your back and scream—
'O Lawk! O criky! It's a dream!'

*

John Aubrey
The Natural History of Wiltshire (1691)

The garden at Lavington in this county, and that at Chelsey in Middlesex, as likewise the house there, doe remaine monuments of [Sir John Danvers's] ingenuity. The garden at Lavington is full of irregularities, both naturall and artificiall, sc. elevations and depressions. Through the length of it there runneth a fine clear trowt stream; walled with brick on each side, to hinder the earth from mouldring down. In this stream are placed severall statues. At the west end there is an admirable place for a grotto, where the great arch is, over which now is the market roade. Among severall others, there is a very pleasant elevation on the south side of the garden, which steales, arising almost insensibly, that is, before one is aware, and gives you a view over the spatious corn-fields there, and so to East Lavington: where, being landed on a fine levell, letteth you descend again with the like easinesse; each side is flanqued with laurels. It is almost impossible to describe this garden, it is so full of variety and unevenesse; nay, it would be a difficult matter for a good artist to make a draught of it.

*

Tobias Smollett
Humphrey Clinker (1771)

Imagine to yourself, my dear Letty, a spacious garden, part laid out in delightful walks, bounded with high hedges and trees, and paved with gravel; part exhibiting a wonderful assemblage of the most picturesque and striking objects, pavilions, lodges, groves, grottoes, lawns, temples, and cascades; porticoes, colonnades, and rotundos; adorned with pillars, statues, and painting; the whole illuminated with an infinite number of lamps, disposed in different figures of suns, stars and constellations; the place crowded with the gayest company, ranging through those blissful shades, or supping in different lodges on cold collations, enlivened with mirth, freedom, and good humour, and animated by an excellent band of music. I had the happiness to hear the celebrated Mrs.—, whose voice was so loud and so shrill that it made my head ache through an excess of pleasure.

*

Sir Roy Strong
A Celebration of Gardens (1991)

The first person who ever seriously walked me round a garden was Cecil Beaton. I remember those weekends at Reddish House as a revelation in living expressed through creativity in both house and garden. After lunch he would put a broad-brimmed hat on his head and out we would go. First on to the terrace where pink roses jostled in profusion through the balustrading and up the rear façade of the house. The land rose steeply away from it towards Edwardian rope rose garlands looking as though they had been lifted from a stage set for Lily Elsie. Our route would not be there but away from the house to one side across a broad sweep of perfectly kept lawn, the pride of Smallpeice the gardener. The garden was held within a hollow, the high perimeters of which had handsome old trees curtaining the cultivated area within. Our walk would take us boldly across the greensward and up towards two huge herbaceous borders framing a stone path ending with a comfortable wooden seat. In summer those borders were magnificent with huge clumps of *Crambe cordifolia* with its star-like white flowers waving in the background. We would then turn sharp right to admire roses trained flat over frames, and then on down through a small paved garden of lavender nestling at the foot of a sundial and back past a wide shrub border. In spring that border was full of purple lilac and one left the house with huge armfuls to sit embowered on the train back to London.

*

Rudyard Kipling
"The Glory of the Garden" from C. R. L. Fletcher's *A History of England* (1911)

Our England is a garden that is full of stately views,
Of borders, beds and shrubberies and lawns and avenues,
With statues on the terraces and peacocks strutting by,
But the Glory of the Garden lies in more than meets the eye.

For where the old thick laurels grow, along the thin red
wall,
You find the tool- and potting-sheds which are the heart of
all;
The cold-frames and the hot-houses, the dungpits and the
tanks,
The rollers, carts and drain-pipes, with the barrows and the
planks.

And there you'll see the gardeners, the men and 'prentice
boys
Told off to do as they are bid and do it without noise:
For, except when seeds are planted and we shout to scare the
birds
The Glory of the Garden it abideth not in words.

And some can pot begonias and some can bud a rose,
And some are hardly fit to trust with anything that grows;
But they can roll and trim the lawns and sift the sand
and loam,
For the Glory of the Garden occupieth all who come.
Our England is a garden, and such gardens are not made
By singing:—'Oh, how beautiful!' and sitting in the shade,

While better men than we go out and start their working
    lives
At grubbing weeds from gravel-paths with broken dinner-
    knives.

There's not a pair of legs so thin, there's not a head so thick,
There's not a hand so weak and white, nor yet a heart
    so sick,
But it can find some needful job that's crying to be done,
For the Glory of the Garden glorifieth every one.

    Then seek your job with thankfulness and work till further
orders,
    If it's only netting strawberries or killing slugs on
borders;
    And when your back stops aching and your hands begin
to harden,
    You will find yourself a partner in the Glory of the
Garden.

    Oh, Adam was a gardener, and God who made him sees
    That half a proper gardener's work is done upon his
knees,
    So when your work is finished, you can wash your hands
and pray
    For the Glory of the Garden, that it may not pass away!
    And the Glory of the Garden it shall never pass away!

*

E. M. Forster
Howard's End (1910)

Then the car turned away, and it was as if a curtain had risen. For the second time that day she saw the appearance of the earth.

There were the greengage trees that Helen had once described, there the tennis lawn, there the hedge that would be glorious with dog-roses in June, but the vision now was of black and palest green. Down by the dell-hole more vivid colours were awakening, and Lent lilies stood sentinel on its margins, or advanced in battalions over the grass. Tulips were a tray of jewels. She could not see the wych-elm tree, but a branch of the celebrated vine, studded with velvet knobs, had covered the porch. She was struck by the fertility of the soil; she had seldom been in a garden where the flowers looked so well, and even the weeds she was idly plucking out of the porch were intensely green. Why had poor Mr Bryce fled from all this beauty? For she had already decided that the place was beautiful.

*

Sir William Temple
Upon the Gardens of Epicurus; or Gardening in the Year 1685 (1692)

The perfectest figure of a garden I ever saw*, either at home or abroad, was that of Moor-Park in Hertfordshire, when I knew it about thirty years ago....Because I take [it] to have been in all kinds the most beautiful and perfect, at least in the figure and disposition that I have ever seen, I will describe it for a model to those that meet with such a situation, and

* See page 113

are above the regards of common expence. It lies on the side of a hill, upon which the house stands, not very steep. The length of the house, where the best rooms and of most use or pleasure are, lies upon the breadth of the garden; the great parlour opens into the middle of a terras gravel-walk that lies even with it, and which may lie, as I remember, about three hundred paces long, and broad in proportion; the border set with standard laurels and at large distances, which have the beauty of orange-trees out of flower and fruit. From this walk there are three descents by many stone steps, in the middle and at each end, into a very large parterre. This is divided into quarters by gravel-walks, and adorned with two fountains and eight statues in the several quarters. At the end of the terras-walk are two summer-houses, and the sides of the parterre are ranged with two large cloisters open to the garden, upon arches of stone, and ending with two other summer-houses even with the cloisters, which are paved with stone, and designed for walks of shade, there being none other in the whole parterre. Over these two cloisters are two terrasses covered with lead and fenced with balusters; and the passage into these airy walks is out of the two summer-houses at the end of the first terras-walk. The cloister facing the south is covered with vines, and would have been proper for an orange-house, and the other for myrtles or other more common greens, and had, no doubt, been cast for that purpose, if this piece of gardening had been then as much in vogue as it is now.

From the middle of this parterre is a descent by many steps flying on each side of a grotto that lies between them, covered with lead and flat, into the lower garden, which is all fruit trees ranged about the several quarters of a wilderness which is very shady; the walks here are all green, the grotto embellished with figures of shell-rock-work, fountains, and water-works. If the hill had not ended with the lower garden, and the wall were not bounded by a common way that goes through the park, they might have added a third quarter of all greens; but this want is supplied by a garden on the other side of the house, which is all of that sort, very wild, shady, and adorned with rough rock-work and fountains.

This was Moor-park, when I was acquainted with it, and the sweetest place, I think, that I have seen in my life, either before or since, at home.

*

Ivan Turgenev
A House of Gentlefolk (1858)
Translated by Constance Garnett

Having looked over the house, Lavretsky went into the garden and was very much pleased with it. It was all overgrown with high grass, and burdock, and gooseberry and raspberry bushes, but there was plenty of shade, and many old lime trees, which were quite remarkable for their immense size and the peculiar growth of their branches; they had been planted too close and at some time or other—a hundred years before— they had been lopped. At the end of the garden was a small clear pool bordered with high reddish rushes. The traces of human life very quickly! pass away; Glafira Petrovna's estate had not had time to become quite wild, but already it seemed plunged in that quiet slumber in which everything reposes on earth where there is not the infection of man's restlessness.

*

Charles Dickens
Bleak House (1853)

He lived in a pretty house, formerly the parsonage house, with a lawn in front, a bright flower-garden at the side, and a well-stocked orchard and kitchen-garden in the rear, enclosed with a venerable wall that had of itself a ripened ruddy look. But, indeed, everything about the place wore an aspect to maturity and abundance. The old lime-tree walk was like green cloisters, the very shadows of the cherry-trees and apple-trees were heavy with fruit, the gooseberry bushes were so laden that their branches arched and rested on the earth, the strawberries and raspberries grew in like profusion, and the peaches basked by the hundred on the wall. Tumbled about among the spread nets and the glass frames sparkling and winking in the sun there were such heaps of drooping pods, and marrows, and cucumbers, that every foot of the ground appeared a vegetable treasury, while the smell of sweet herbs and all kinds of wholesome growth (to say nothing of the neighbouring meadows where the hay was carrying) made the whole air a great nosegay. Such stillness and composure reigned within the orderly precincts of the old red wall that even the feathers hung in garland to scare the birds hardly stirred; and the wall had such a ripening influence that where, here and there high up, a disused nail and scrap of list still clung to it, it was easy to fancy that they had mellowed with the changing seasons and they had rusted and decayed according to the common faith.

*

Elizabeth von Arnim
Elizabeth and Her German Garden (1898)

Give me a garden full of strong, healthy creatures, able to stand roughness and cold without dismally giving in and dying. I never could see that delicacy of constitution is pretty, either in plants or in women. No doubt there are many lovely flowers to be had by heat and constant coaxing, but then for each of these there are fifty others still lovelier that will gratefully grow in God's wholesome air and are blessed in return with a far greater intensity of scent and colour.

We have been very busy until now getting the permanent beds in order and planting the new tea-roses, and I am looking forward to next summer with more hope than ever in spite of my many failures. I wish the years would pass quickly that will bring my garden to perfection! The Persian Yellows have gone into their new quarters, and their place is occupied by the tea-rose Safrano; all the rose beds are carpeted with pansies sown in July and transplanted in October, each bed having a separate colour. The purple ones are the most charming and go well with every rose, but I have white ones with Laurette Messimy, and yellow ones with Safrano, and a new red sort in the big centre bed of red roses. Round the semicircle on the south side of the little privet hedge two rows of annual larkspurs in all their delicate shades have been sown, and just beyond the larkspurs, on the grass, is a semicircle of standard tea and pillar roses. In front of the house the long borders have been stocked with larkspurs, annual and perennial, columbines, giant poppies, pinks, Madonna lilies, wallflowers, hollyhocks, perennial phloxes, peonies, lavender, starworts, cornflowers, lychnis chalcedonia, and bulbs packed in wherever bulbs could go. These are the borders that were so hardly used by the other gardener. Spring boxes for the veranda steps have been filled with pink and white and yellow tulips. I love tulips better than any other spring flower; they are the embodiment of alert cheerfulness and tidy grace, and next to a hyacinth look like a wholesome, freshly tubbed young girl beside a stout lady whose every movement weighs down the air with patchouli.

*

William Wordsworth
"The White Doe of Rylestone" (1807)

> ...Within this spacious plot
> For pleasure made, a goodly spot,
> With lawns and beds of flowers, and shades
> Of trellis-work in long arcades,
> And cirque and crescent framed by wall
> Of close-clipt foliage green and tall,
> Converging walks, and fountains gay,
> And terraces in trim array—
> Beneath yon cypress spiring high,
> With pine and cedar spreading wide
> Their darksome boughs on either side,
> In open moonlight doth she lie;
> Happy as others of her kind,
> That, far from human neighbourhood,
> Range unrestricted as the wind,
> Through park, or chase, or savage wood.

*

Alexander Pope
Letter to Edward Blount (June 2, 1725)

Let the young Ladies be assured I make nothing new in my Gardens without wishing to see the print of their Fairy Steps in every part of 'em. I have put the last Hand to my works of this kind, in happily finishing the subterraneous Way and Grotto; I there found a spring of the clearest Water, which falls in a perpetual Rill, that echoes thro' the Cavern day and night. From the River *Thames*, you see thro' my Arch up a Walk of the Wilderness to a kind of open Temple, wholly compos'd of Shells in the Rustic Manner; and from that distance under the Temple you look down thro' a sloping Arcade of Trees, and see the Sails on the River passing suddenly and vanishing, as thro' a Perspective Glass...There are connected to this Grotto by a narrower Passage two Porches, with niches and seats, one toward the River, of smooth Stones, full of light and open; the other toward the Arch of Trees, rough with Shells, Flints, and Iron Ore. The Bottom is paved with simple Pebble, as the adjoining Walk up the Wilderness to the Temple, is to be Cockle-shells, in the natural Taste, agreeing not ill with the little dripping Murmur, and the Aquatic Idea of the whole Place...You'll think I have been very Poetical in this Description, but it is pretty near the Truth.

*

Po Chü-i
"Planting Flowers on the Eastern Embankment" (819)
Translated by Arthur Waley

I took money and bought flowering trees
And planted them out on the bank to the east of the Keep.
I simply bought whatever had the most blooms,
Not caring whether peach, or apricot, or plum.
A hundred fruits, all mixed up together;
A thousand branches, flowering in due rotation.
Each has its season coming early or late;
But to all alike the fertile soil is kind.
The red flowers hang like a heavy mist;
The white flowers gleam like a fall of snow.
The wandering bees cannot bear to leave them;
The sweet birds also come there to roost.
In front there flows an ever-running stream;
Beneath there is built a little flat terrace.
Sometimes I sweep the flagstones of the terrace;
Sometimes, in the wind, I raise my cup and drink.
The flower branches screen my head from the sun;
The flower-buds fall down into my lap.
Alone drinking, alone singing my songs
I do not notice the moon is level with the steps.
The people of Pa do not care for flowers;
All the spring no one has come to look.
But their Governor General, alone with his cup of wine,
Sits till evening and will not move from the place!

*

Mary Russell Mitford
Letter to Elizabeth Barrett Browning, June 20, 1842

... I write to say that on Saturday next (the very day on which you will receive this) we shall send you some flowers. Oh, how I wish we could transport you into the garden where they grow! You would like it—the '*entourage*', as Mrs Mackie calls it, is so pretty: one side (it is nearly an acre of show flowers) a high hedge of hawthorn, with giant trees rising above it beyond the hedge, whilst all down within the garden are clumps of matchless hollyhocks and splendid dahlias; the top of the garden being shut in by the old irregular cottage, with its dark brickwork covered with vines and roses, and its picturesque chimneys mingling with the bay tree, again rising into its bright and shining cone, and two old pear trees festooned with honeysuckle; the bottom of the garden and the remaining side consisting of lower hedgerows melting into wooded uplands, dotted with white cottages and patches of common. Nothing can well be imagined more beautiful than this little bit of ground is now. Huge masses of lupines (say fifty or sixty spiral spikes), some white, some lilac; immense clumps of the enamelled Siberian larkspur, glittering like some enormous Chinese jar; the white and azure blossoms of the variegated monkshood; flags of all colours; roses of every shade, some covering the house and stables and overtopping the roofs, others mingling with tall apple trees, other again (especially the beautiful double Scotch rose) low but broad, standing in bright relief to the blues and purples; and the oriental poppy, like an orange lamp (for it really seems to have light within it) shining amidst the deeper greens; above all, the pyramid of geraniums, beautiful beyond all beauty, rising in front of our garden room, whilst each corner is filled with the same beautiful flower, and the whole air perfumed by the delicious honeysuckle. Nothing can be more lovely.

*

Henry Fielding
The History of Tom Jones (1729)

The Gothic stile of building could produce nothing nobler that Mr. Allworthy's house. There was an air of grandeur in it that struck you with awe, and rivalled the beauties of the best Grecian architecture; and it was as commodious within as venerable without.

It stood on the south-east side of a hill, but nearer the bottom than the top of it, so as to be sheltered from the north-east by a grove of old oaks which rose above it in a gradual ascent of near half a mile, and yet high enough to enjoy a most charming prospect of the valley beneath.

In the midst of the grove was a fine lawn, sloping down towards the house, near the summit of which rose a plentiful spring, gushing out of a rock covered with firs, and forming a constant cascade of about thirty feet, not carried down a regular flight of steps, but tumbling in natural fall over the broken and mossy stones till it came to the bottom of the rock, then running off in a pebbly channel, that with many lesser falls winded along, till it fell into a lake at the foot of the hill, about a quarter of a mile below the house on the south side, and which was seen from every room in the front. Out of this lake, which filled the centre of a beautiful plain, embellished with groups of beeches and elms, and fed with sheep, issued a river, that for several miles was seen to meander through an amazing variety of meadows and woods till it emptied itself into the sea, with a large arm of which, and an island beyond it, the prospect was closed.

On the right of this valley opened another of less extent, adorned with several villages, and terminated by one of the towers of an old ruined abbey, grown over with ivy, and part of the front, which remained still entire.

The left-hand scne presented the view of a very fine park, composed of very unequal ground, and agreeably varied with all the diversity that hills, lawns, wood, and water, laid out with admirable taste, but owing les to art than to nature, could give. Beyond this, the country gradually rose into a ridge of wild mountains, the tops of which were above the clouds.

It was now the middle of May, and the morning was remarkably serene, when Mr Allworthy walked forth on the terrace, where the dawn opened every minute that lovely prospect we have before described to his eye; and now having sent forth streams of light, which ascended the blue firmament before him, as harbingers preceding his pomp, in the full blaze of his majesty rose the sun, than which one object alone in this lower creation could be more glorious, and that Mr Allworthy himself presented—a human being replete with benevolence, meditating in what manner he might render himself most acceptable to his Creator, by doing most good to his creatures.

*

Emily Carr

The House of All Sorts (1944)

From the front of the house you got no hint that it contained the finest studio in the town. The tell-tale great north light was at the back of the house and overlooked my own garden, dominating its every corner. There were open fields surrounding my garden—fields that were the playgrounds of my Bobtail Sheep-dogs, kennelled behind the lilacs and apple-trees at the foot of the garden. It was not a very large garden, centred by a lawn which again was centred by a great olivet cherry tree. In the crotch of the tree a shelter box was fixed for the comfort of my monkey, Woo, during the summer months.

The garden was fenced and gated. It belonged exclusively to the animals and myself. No one intruded there. Visitors or tenants who came to pay or to grumble mounted the long outside stair that met the paved walk on the west side of the house, and took their complaints to me in the studio. People came to see me on business; if I wanted to see myself I went to the garden. If I was angry I seized a spade and dug my anger into the soil. When I was sad the garden earth swallowed my tears, when I was merry the garden lawn danced with bouncing dogs, monkey, the Persian cat, Adolphus, and me. We did have good times in that old garden.

*

Thomas Sheridan
"A Description of Dr. Delaney's Villa" (1722–23)

> ...Next come I to your kitchen-garden,
> Where one poor mouse would fare but hard in;
> And round this garden is a walk,
> No longer than a tailor's chalk;
> Thus I compare what space is in it,
> *A snail creeps round it in a minute.*
> One lettuce makes a shift to squeeze
> Up through the tuft you call your trees;
> And, once a year, a single rose
> Peeps from the bud, but never blows;
> In vain then you expect its bloom!
> It cannot blow for want of room.
>
> "In short, for all your boasted seat,
> There's nothing *but yourself that's great!*"

*

Jane Austen
Pride and Prejudice (1813)

After sitting long enough to admire every article of furniture in the room, from the sideboard to the fender, to give an account of their journey, and of all that had happened in London, Mr. Collins invited them to take a stroll in the garden, which was large and well laid out, and to the cultivation of which he attended himself. To work in his garden was one of his most respectable pleasures; and Elizabeth admired the command of countenance with which Charlotte talked of the healthfulness of the exercise, and owned she encouraged it as much as possible. Here, leading the way through every walk and cross walk, and scarcely allowing them an interval to utter the praises he asked for, every view was pointed out with a minuteness which left beauty entirely behind. He could number the fields in every direction, and could tell how many trees there were in the most distant clump. But of all the views which his garden, or which the country or the kingdom could boast, none were to be compared with the prospect of Rosings, afforded by an opening in the trees that bordered the park nearly opposite the front of his house. It was a handsome modern building, well *situated* on rising ground.

John Galt
The Last of the Lairds: or, The Life and Opinions of Malachi Mailings, Esq. (1826)

The garden was suitable to the offices and the mansion. It was surrounded, but not inclosed, by an undressed hedge, which in more than fifty places offered tempting admission to the cows. The luxuriant grass walks were never mowed but just before hay time, and every stock of kail and cabbage stood in its garmentry of curled blades, like a new-made Glasgow baillie's wife on the first Sunday after Michaelmas, dressed for the kirk in the many-plies of all her flounces. Clumps of apple-ringie, daisies and Dutch admirals, marigolds and nonsopretties, jonquils and gillyflowers, with here and there a peony, a bunch of gardeners-garters, a sunflower or an orange-lily, mingled their elegant perfumes and delicate flourishes along the borders. The fruit-trees were of old renown; none grew sweeter pears; and if the apples were not in co-rival estimation with the palate, they were yet no less celebrated for the rural beauty of their red cheeks. It is true, that the cherries were dukes, but the plumbs were magnuminums.

Where the walks met stood a gnomonless dial; opposite to which, in a honey-suckle bower, a white-painted seat invited the Laird's visitors of a sentimental turn to read Hervey's *Meditations in a Flower-garden*; and there, in the still moonlight nights, in the nightingale-singing season of southern climes, you might overhear one of the servant lasses keckling with her sweetheart. But it is time to approach the house, and make our way towards the inmates.

FAR AWAY

There is a category of literary gardens whose charm and
curiosity lies in their remoteness. To some extent this is the
realm of travel writers reporting from foreign parts on the
strange things they find there. But in the finest examples we
get a piercing sense of psychological strangeness to match
the physical distance. Lafcadio Hearn in a Japanese garden
built of sand and stone, Sir Robert Ker Porter in the water-
garden of a Persian palace, even Scott Fitzgerald describing
the contrasts of dry and lush in a garden on the Côte d'Azur
all suggest how much there is beyond the familiar, how wide
the world.

Time too sets gardens apart. The garden of Alcinous in
the *Odyssey* or Sir Thomas Browne's seventeenth century
description of Paradise ('Gardens were before Gardiners') are

as remote as the pavilion-studded Peking garden where Cao Xueqin's characters contemplated lotuses and wrote poems. Yet they are nonetheless all a part of a great gardening tradition, one with many branches.

Robert Byron
The Architectural Review (1931)

Of the Garden itself [The Viceroy's Garden New Delhi], some 12 acres in extent—of its maze of grass squares, flower beds, and bridged waters at different levels, all framed in the red stone; of it fountains like heaps of pennies; of its exquisite red and white gazebos, whose pierced panels are repeated in the water beside them; of the terraced battlements of flowers than rise like bastions on either side; of the stone Eiffel towers at the ends, bound in flashing brass and awaiting the growth of the trees inside them; of the stone hoops along the further boundary; of the stone pergola in the corridor beyond; and of the final circular enclosure attached to the corridor as a racquet to its handle, many pages could be written, and will be elsewhere. The general effect, at present, is bare; but in ten years the existing trees will have become a forest. The design, like the elaborate and formal water systems of the Moguls and the Italians, is strictly architectural, and is thus made the instrument of a logical transition between the great house behind and the rough landscape overlooked. But this process is not accomplished by them alone. Far out in the landscaper itself lie, on one side, the Viceroy's stables, and on the other, the Viceroy's body-guard lines: complicated and symmetrical groups of buildings, having towers at their ends, and so planned, diamond-wise, as to accentuate their diagonal relation to the central axis—the axis which persists from the Memorial Arch at the foot of the King's Way to the centre of the garden's final pond in the circular enclosure beyond the corridor. Thus, if the Viceroy steps out to pick a rose, he can look up to find the very horizon in deferential alignment with himself. Such is a proper setting for a ruler. But the architect has given his heart to the pansies as well. Throughout the garden is visible the same consummate manipulation of stone as distinguishes the whole city. Even the flowers have responded to the environment of perfection.

*

Lu You (1125-1210)
"Small Garden"
Translated by Stephen Owen

Misty plants of my small garden
reach to my neighbor's home,
and through the shade of mulberries
a single path slants.
I lay here reading Tao Qian's poems,
but before I finished the book,
I took advantage of gentle rain
to go and weed my melons.

*

Sir Robert Ker Porter
Travels in Georgia, Persia, Armenia and Ancient Babylon during the Years 1817, 1818, 1819, and 1820 (1821)

One of the most delicious spots to which I paid the most frequent visits, after the commencement of the genial weather I speak of, was the garden of Negauristan, another palace of the king's.... The general character of the garden, is like that of Tackt-i-kajer, only the grand avenue up the centre of this, is much wider than that of the more distant residence, and is terminated at the higher extremity by a view of the palace; while a Kooleh Frangy, or temple, appears here also between the spacious arcade of trees. Narrow secluded walks, shaded above, and enamelled with flowers below, with cuts of clear and sparkling water, silvering the ground, and cooling the air, vary the scene, from parts of which the hand of neglect (or taste, assuming graceful negligence) has left in a state of romantic wilderness. The trees were nearly all full grown, and luxuriant in foliage; while their lofty stems, nearly covered by a rich underwood of roses, lilacs, and other fragrant and aromatic shrubs, formed the finest natural tapestry of leaves and flowers.

On my first entering this bower of fairyland (indeed I may call it the very garden of Beauty and the Beast!) I was struck with the appearance of two rose-trees, full fourteen feet high, laden with thousands of flowers, in every degree of expansion, and of a bloom and delicacy of scent, that imbued the whole atmosphere with the most exquisite perfume. Indeed, I believe that in no country of the world does the rose grow in such perfection as in Persia; in no country is it so cultivated, and prized by the natives. Their gardens and courts are crowded with its plants, their rooms ornamented with vases, filled with its gathered bunches, and every bath is strewn with the full-blown flowers, plucked from the ever replenished stems. Even the humblest individual, who pays a piece of copper money for a few whiffs of a kalion, feels a double enjoyment when he finds it stuck with a bud from his dear native tree. But in this delicious garden of Negauristan, the eye and the smell were not the only senses regaled by the presence of roses. The ear was enchanted by the wild and beautiful notes of multitudes of nightingales, whose warbling seemed to increase in melody and softness, with the unfolding of their favourite flowers; verifying the song of the poet, who says: 'When the roses fade, when the charms of the bower are passed away, the fond tale of the nightingale no longer animates the scene.'

*

Cao Xueqin
Hung Lou Meng (Dream of the Red Chamber)
Translated by David Hawkes under the title *The Story of the Stone*

As he spoke, he entered the cave, where he perceived beautiful trees with thick foliage, quaint flowers in lustrous bloom, while a line of limpid stream emanated out of a deep recess among the flowers and trees, and oozed down through the crevice of the rock. Progressing several steps further in, they gradually faced the northern side, where a stretch of level ground extended far and wide, on each side of which soared lofty buildings, intruding themselves into the skies, whose carved rafters and engraved balustrades nestled entirely among the depressions of the hills and the tops of the trees. They lowered their eyes and looked, and beheld a pure stream flowing like jade, stone steps traversing the clouds, a balustrade of white marble encircling the pond in its embrace, and a stone bridge with three archways, the animals upon which had faces disgorging water from their mouths. A pavilion stood on the bridge, and in this pavilion Chia Chen and the whole party went and sat.

—

Pao-yü cast a glance round the four quarters, when an idea came into his head, and he went on to recite:

The willows, which enclose the shore, the green borrow
from three bamboos;
On banks apart, the flowers asunder grow, yet one
perfume they give.

Upon hearing these lines, Chia Cheng gave a faint smile, as he nodded his head, whilst the whole party went on again to be effusive in their praise. But forthwith they issued from the pavilions, and crossed the pond, contemplating with close attention each elevation, each stone, each flower, or each tree. And as suddenly they raised their heads, they caught sight, in front of them, of a line of white wall, of numbers of columns, and beautiful cottages, where flourished hundreds and thousands of verdant bamboos, which screened off the rays of the sun.

"What a lovely place!" they one and all exclaimed.

Speedily the whole company penetrated inside, perceiving, as soon as they had entered the gate, a zigzag arcade, below the steps of which was a raised pathway, laid promiscuously with stones, and on the furthest part stood a diminutive cottage with three rooms, two with doors leading into them and one without. Everything in the interior, in the shape of beds, teapoys, chairs and tables, were made to harmonise with the space available. Leading out of the inner room of the cottage was a small door from which, as they egressed, they found a back-court with lofty pear trees in blossom and banana trees, as well as two very small retiring back-courts. At the foot of the wall, unexpectedly became visible an aperture where was a spring, for which a channel had been opened scarcely a foot or so wide, to enable it to run inside the wall. Winding round the steps, it skirted the buildings until it reached the front court, where it coiled and curved, flowing out under the bamboos.

'This spot,' observed Chia Cheng full of smiles, 'is indeed pleasant! and could one, on a moonlight night, sit under the window and study, one would not spend a whole lifetime in vain!'

*

Sir Thomas Browne
The Garden of Cyrus (1658)

If Paradise were planted the third day of the Creation, as wiser Divinity concludeth, the Nativity thereof was too early for Horoscopy; Gardens were before Gardiners, and but some hours after the earth.

Of deeper doubt is its Topography, and local designation, yet being the primitive garden, and without much controversie situated in the East; it is more than probable the first curiosity, and cultivation of plants, most flourished in those quarters. And since the Ark of *Noah* first touched upon some mountains of *Armenia*, the planting art arose again in the East, and found its revolution not far from the place of its Nativity, about the Plains of those Regions.

*

Lafcadio Hearn

Glimpses of Unfamiliar Japan (1894)

I do not know what human sentiment the principal division of my garden was intended to reflect; and there is none to tell me. Those by whom it was made passed away long generations ago, in the eternal migration of souls. But as a poem of nature it requires no interpreter. It occupies the front portion of the grounds, facing south; and it also extends west to the verge of the northern division of the garden, from which it is partially separated by a curious screen-fence structure. There are large rocks in it, heavily mossed; and divers fantastic basins of stone for holding water; and stone lamps green with years; and a shachihoko, such as one sees at the peaked angles of castle roofs—a great stone fish, an idealised porpoise, with its nose in the ground and its tail in the air. There are miniature hills, with old trees upon them; and there are long slopes of green, shadowed by flowering shrubs, like river banks; and there are green knolls like islets. All these verdant elevations rise from spaces of pale yellow sand, smooth as the surface of silk and miming the curves and meandering of a river course. These sanded spaces are not to be trodden upon; they are much too beautiful for that. These least speck of dirt would mar their effect; and it requires the trained skill of an experienced native gardener—a delightful old man he is—to keep them in perfect form. But they are traversed in various directions by lines of flat, unhewn rock slabs, placed at slightly irregular distances from one another, exactly like stepping stones across a brook. The whole effect is that of the shores of a still stream in some lovely, lonesome, drowsy place.

*

Tanizaki Junichirō

The Makioka Sisters (1957) Translated by Edward Seidensticker

Etsuko started back to school after a day's rest. Sachiko, on the other hand, only felt more exhausted. She would call in a masseuse and lie down for a nap in the middle of the day, or she would go out to sit on the terrace.

Perhaps because it reflected the tastes of one who preferred spring, the garden had little in it to attract the eye; a rather forlorn hibiscus in the shade of the hillock, and a clump of *hagi* [*Lespedeza japonica*] trailing its white flowers off toward the Stoltz fence. The sandalwood and the plane trees, such a profusion of leaves in summertime, were limp and tired. The green of the lawn was much as it had been when she left, and yet the sun seemed a little weaker. The garden carried just a suggestion of coolness, the smell of a sweet olive reminded her that in Ashiya too autumn was near. They would soon have to take in the reed awning. These last two or three days she had felt an intense affection for the familiar garden. It was good to go away now and then. Possibly because she was not used to travelling, she felt that she had been away at least a month. She remembered how Yukiko treasured every minute, how she would walk through the garden, stopping here and there, when she had to go back to Tokyo. Yukiko was not the only child of Osaka, Sachiko knew. This was a most unremarkable little garden, but even here, smelling the pines, looking at the mountains and the clear sky, she thought there could be no finer place to live than the suburbs of Osaka. How unpleasant Tokyo was, how dusty, grey, pushing. Yukiko was fond of saying that the very feel of Osaka air was different, and she was right.

*

Homer
The Odyssey

Beyond the courtyard, near to the doors, lies a large four-acre orchard, surrounded by a hedge. Tall, heavily-laden trees grow there, pear, pomegranate and apple, rich in glossy fruit, sweet figs and dense olives. The fruit never rots or fails, winter or summer. It lasts all year, and the West Wind's breath quickens some to life, and ripens others, pear on pear, apple on apple, cluster on cluster of grapes, and fig on fig. There is Alcinous's fertile vineyard too, with a warm patch of level ground in one part set aside for drying the grapes, while the labourers gather and tread others, as the foremost rows of unripe grapes shed their blossom, and other become tinged with purple. Beyond the furthest row again are neat beds with every kind of plant, flowering all year round, and there are two springs in the orchard, one flowing through the whole garden, while the other runs the opposite way, under the courtyard sill, near where the people of the city draw their water, towards the great house. Such were the gods' glorious gifts to Alcinous's home.

*

D. J. Enright
"A Kyoto Garden" from *Collected Poems* (1956)

Here you could pass your holidays,
    trace and retrace the turning ways,
a hundred yards of stepping stones, you feel
    yourself a traveller, alone.

you skirt a range of moss, you cross
    and cross again what seems new Rubicons,
a tan of land will make ten prefectures,
    a tideless pond a great pacific sea.

each vista, you remark, seems the intended prize—
    like Fuji through a spider's web or else
between a cooper's straining thighs—
    the eyes need never be averted, nor the nose;

across a two-foot fingered canyon, an Amazon of dew,
    a few dwarf maples
lose you in a forest, then you gain a mole-hill's
    panoramic view,

and company enough, a large anthology—
    the golden crow, the myriad leaves,
the seven autumn flowers, the seven herbs of spring,
    the moon sends down a rice-cake and a cassia-tree—

till under a sliding foot a pebble shrieks:
    you hesitate—
what feeds this corpulent moss, whose emptied blood,
    what demon mouths await?—

but then you notice that the pines wear crutches—
    typhoons show no respect for art or craft;
you sigh with happiness, the garden comes alive:
    like us, these princelings feel the draught.

*

F. Scott Fitzgerald
Tender is the Night (1934)

Feeling good from the rosy wine at lunch, Nicole Diver folded her arms high enough for the artificial camellia on her shoulder to touch her cheek, and went out into her lovely grassless garden. The garden was bounded on one side by the house, from which it flowed and into which it ran, on two sides by the old village, and on the last by the cliff falling by ledges to the sea.

Along the walls on the village side all was dusty, the wriggling vines, the lemon and eucalyptus trees, the casual wheel-barrow, left only a moment since, but already grown into the path, atrophied and faintly rotten. Nicole was invariably somewhat surprised that by turning in the other direction past a bed of peonies she walked into an area so green and cool that the leaves and petals were curled with tender damp...

Following a walk marked by an intangible mist of bloom that followed the white border stones she came to a space overlooking the sea where there were lanterns asleep in the fig trees and a big table and wicker chairs and a great market umbrella from Siena, all gathered about an enormous pine, the biggest tree in the garden. She paused there a moment, looking absently at a growth of nasturtiums and iris tangled at its foot, as though sprung from a careless handful of seeds, listening to the plaints and accusations of some nursery squabble in the house. When this died away on the summer air, she walked on, between kaleidoscopic peonies massed in pink clouds, black and brown tulips and fragile mauve-stemmed roses, transparent like sugar flowers in a confectioner's window—until, as if the scherzo of color could reach no further intensity, it broke off suddenly in mid-air, and moist steps went down to a level five feet below.

Here there was a well with the boarding around it dank and slippery even on the brightest days. She went up the stairs on the other side and into the vegetable garden; she walked rather quickly; she liked to be active, though at times she gave an impression of repose that was at once static and evocative. This was because she knew few words and believed in none, and in the world she was rather silent, contributing just her share of urbane humor with a precision that approached meagreness. But at the moment when strangers tended to grow uncomfortable in the presence of this economy she would seize the topic and rush off with it, feverishly surprised with herself—and then bring it back and relinquish it abruptly, almost timidly, like and obedient retriever, having been adequate and something more.

As she stood in the fuzzy green light of the vegetable garden, Dick crossed the path ahead of her going to his work house. Nicole waited silently until he had passed; then she went on through lines of prospective salads to a little menagerie where pigeons and rabbits and a parrot made a medley of insolent noises at her. Descending to another ledge she reached a low curved wall and looked down seven hundred feet to the Mediterranean Sea.

SCEPTICISM

There are, let's face it, some writers who are less than keen about gardens. Samuel Johnson is one—his famous quip on gardening ('It must at least be confessed, that to embellish the form of nature is an innocent amusement') is memorable if not necessarily fair. Others are quick to express their doubts about particular gardens while not writing off the whole practice. After all, opinions differ here as in most human pursuits. Mark Twain, for example, finds something to admire in the regimented topiary of Versailles while dismissing the homegrown American version. Where Sir William Temple found Moor Park to be 'the perfectest figure of a garden I ever saw', the poet William Mason is scathing about it. And Anthony Trollope makes plain his limited admiration for the gardens of *The Small House at Allington,* although the estate woods are blessedly full of foxes.

Sometimes it is a cultural matter. Mary Wollstonecraft, visiting a Norwegian version of an English garden, decides that it would be far more satisfactory as a Norwegian garden. As for Jerome K. Jerome's *Three Men in a Boat*, taking a dry land break at Hampton Court in order to explore the maze, the garden itself is scarcely the issue—the main problem, barely solved in the end, is how to find their way out. Garden writing or not, it's a passage to prize.

Samuel Johnson

The Lives of the Poets (on William Shenstone's Leasowes) (1781)

Now was excited his delight in rural pleasures, and his ambition of rural elegance: he began, from this time, to point his prospects, to diversify his surface, to entangle his walks, and to wind his waters; which he did with such judgement and such fancy, as made his little domain the envy of the great, and the admiration of the skilful; a place to be visited by travellers, and copied by designers. Whether to plant a walk in undulating curves, and to place a bench at every turn where there is an object to catch the view; to make water run where it will be heard, and to stagnate where it will be seen; to leave intervals where the eye will be pleased, and to thicken the plantation where there is something to be hidden; demands any great powers of mind, I will not inquire: perhaps a surly and sullen speculator may think such performances rather the sport than the business of human reason. But it must be at least confessed, that to embellish the form of nature is an innocent amusement; and some praise must be allowed, by the most supercilious observer, to him who does best what such multitudes are contending to do well.

*

Robert Southey

The Doctor &c. (1834-1847)

The fashion which this buxom Flora introduced had at one time the effect of banishing flowers from what should have been the flower-garden; the ground was set with box in their stead, disposed in patterns more or less formal, some intricate as a labyrinth and not little resembling those of turkey carpets, where Mahommedan laws interdict the likeness of any living thing, and the taste of Turkish weavers excludes any combination of graceful forms. One sense at least was gratified when fragrant herbs were used in these "rare figures of composures," or knots as they were called, hyssop being mixed in them with thyme, as aiders the one to the other, the one being dry, the other moist. Box had the disadvantage of a disagreeable odour; but it was greener in the winter and more compact in all seasons. To lay out these knots and tread them required the skill of a master-gardener: much labour was thus expended without producing any beauty. The walks between them were sometimes of different colours; some would be of lighter or darker gravel, red or yellow sand: and when such materials were at hand, pulverised coal and pulverised shells.

Such a garden Mr. Cradock saw at Bordeaux no longer ago than the year 1785; it belonged to Monsieur Rabi, a very rich Jewish merchant, and was surrounded by a bank of earth, on which there stood about two hundred blue and white flower pots; the garden itself was a scroll-work cut very narrow and the interstices filled with sand of different colours to imitate embroidery; it required repairing after every shower, and if the wind rose, the eyes were sure to suffer. Yet the French admire this and exclaimed, *Superbe! Magnifique!*

*

Tobias Smollett
Travels through France and Italy (1765)

DEAR SIR,—In my last I gave you my opinion freely of the modern palaces of Italy. I shall now hazard my thoughts upon the gardens of this country, which the inhabitants extol with all the hyperboles of admiration and applause...

In a fine extensive garden or park, an Englishman expects to see a number of groves and glades, intermixed with an agreeable negligence, which seems to be the effect of nature and accident. He looks for shady walks encrusted with gravel; for open lawns covered with verdure as smooth as velvet, but much more lively and agreeable; for ponds, canals, basins, cascades, and running streams of water; for clumps of trees, woods, and wildernesses, cut into delightful alleys, perfumed with honeysuckle and sweet-briar, and resounding with the mingled melody of all the singing birds of heaven. He looks for plats of flowers in different parts to refresh the sense, and please the fancy; for arbours, grottos, hermitages, temples, and alcoves, to shelter him from the sun, and afford him means of contemplation and repose; and he expects to find the hedges, groves, and walks, and lawns kept with the utmost order and propriety. He who loves the beauties of simple nature, and the charms of neatness, will seek for them in vain amidst the groves of Italy. In the garden of the Villa Pinciana, there is a plantation of four hundred pines, which the Italians view with rapture and admiration; there is likewise a long walk of trees extending from the garden-gate to the palace; and plenty of shade, with alleys and hedges in different parts of the ground: but the groves are neglected; the walks are laid with nothing but common mould or sand, black and dusty; the hedges are tall, thin and shabby; the trees stunted; the open ground, brown and parched, has scarce any appearance of verdure. The flat, regular alleys of evergreens are cut into fantastic figures; the flower gardens embellished with thin ciphers and flourished figures in box, while the flowers grow in rows of earthern pots, and the ground appears as dusky as if it was covered with the cinders of a blacksmith's forge. The water, of which there is great plenty, instead of being collected in large pieces, or conveyed in little rivulets and streams to refresh the thirsty soil, or managed so as to form agreeable cascades, is squirted from fountains in different parts of the garden, though tubes little bigger and common glyster-pipes. It must be owned indeed that the fountains have their merit in the way of sculpture and architecture; and that there is a great number of statues which merit attention: but they serve only to encumber the ground, and destroy that effect of rural simplicity, which our gardens are designed to produce. In a word, here we see a variety of walks and groves and fountains, a wood of four hundred pines, a paddock with a few meagre deer, a flower-garden, an aviary, a grotto, and a fish-pond; and in spite of all these particulars, it is, in my opinion, a very contemptible garden, when compared to that of Stowe in Buckinghamshire, or even to those of Kensington and Richmond. The Italians understand, because they study, the excellences of art; but they have no idea of the beauties of nature.

*

Mark Twain
Innocents Abroad (1869)

I always thought ill of people at home who trimmed their shrubbery into pyramids and squares and spires and all manner of unnatural shapes, and when I saw the same thing being practiced in this great park [of Versailles] I began to feel dissatisfied. But soon I saw the idea of the thing and the wisdom of it. They seek the general effect. We distort a dozen sickly trees into unaccustomed shapes in a little yard no bigger than a dining room, and then surely they look absurd enough. But here they take two hundred thousand tall forest trees and set them in a double row; allow no sign of leaf or branch to grow on the trunk lower down than six feet above the ground; from that point the boughs begin to project, and very gradually they extend outward further and further till they meet overhead, and a faultless tunnel of foliage is formed. The arch is mathematically precise. The effect is then very fine. They make trees take fifty different shapes, and so these quaint effects are infinitely varied and picturesque. The trees in no two avenues are shaped alike, and consequently the eye is not fatigued with anything in the nature of monotonous uniformity. I will drop this subject now, leaving it to others to determine how these people manage to make endless ranks of lofty forest trees grow to just a certain thickness of trunk (say a foot and two-thirds); how they compel one huge limb to spring from the same identical spot on each tree and form the main sweep of the arch; and how all these things are kept in exactly the same condition and in the same exquisite shapeliness and symmetry month after month and year after year—for I have tried to reason out the problem and have failed.

Jane Austen
Mansfield Park (1814)

'It may seem impertinent of me to praise, but I must admire the taste Mrs. Grant has shewn in all this. There is such a quiet simplicity in the plan of the walk! Not too much attempted!'

'Yes,' replied Miss Crawford, carelessly, 'It does very well for a place of this sort. One does not think of extent *here*; and between ourselves, till I came to Mansfield, I had not imagined a country parson ever aspired to a shrubbery, or anything of the kind.'

'I am so glad to see the evergreens thrive!' said Fanny, in reply. 'My uncle's gardener always says the soil is better here than his own, and so it appears from the growth of the laurels and evergreens in general. The evergreen! When one thinks of it, how astonishing a variety of nature! In some countries we know that the tree that sheds its leaf is the variety, but that does not make it less amazing, that the same soil and the same sun should nurture plants differing in the first rule and law of their existence.'

*

Elizabeth Bowen
'Shoes: an International Episode' from *Collected Stories* (1980)

They were lunching half out of doors, under a roof that covered part of the garden. Now and then, lizards flickered over the tiles at their feet. Just beyond, shadows came to an end with an edge like metal; there was a glare of gravel, palm trees leaned languid together, creeper poured flaming over a wall, and a row of young orange trees in bright glazed vases swaggered along a balustrade. Balanced in the hot stillness, the green glass balls on the wall-top snatched one's attention with their look of precariousness. At the garden's end, impermanent yellow buildings, fit to go down in a puff; intense and feverish, like a memory of Van Gogh's. A long cat, slipping from vase to vase, fawned on its reflection in an unnatural ecstacy.

Dillie looked at all this, sideways. 'You do like this?' said Edward, anxious.

✻

William Mason

"On Temple's praise of Moor Park", *The English Garden* (1771) ✻

> Go to the proof! Behold what TEMPLE call'd
> A perfect Garden, There thou shalt not find
> One blade of verdure, but withn aching feet
> From terras down to terras shalt descend,
> Step following step, by tedious flights of stairs:
> On leaden platforms now the noon-day sun
> Shall scorch thee; now the dank arcades of stone
> Shall chill thy fervour; happy if at length
> Thou reach the Orchard, where the sparing turf
> Through equal lines, all centring in a point,
> Yields thee a softer tread.

✻

✻ See page 76

Mary Wollstonecraft
*Letters Written During a Short Residence in Sweden, Norway,
and Denmark* (1796)

From the fortress I returned to my lodging, and quickly was
taken out of town to be shown a pretty villa, and English
garden. To a Norwegian both might have been objects of
curiosity; and of use, by exciting to the comparison which
leads to improvement. But whilst I gazed, I was employed in
restoring the place to nature, or taste, by giving it the character
of the surrounding scene. Serpentine walks, and flowering-
shrubs, looked trifling in a grand recess of the rooks, shaded
by towering pines. Groves of smaller trees might have been
sheltered under them, which would have melted into the
landscape, displaying only the art which ought to point out
the vicinity of a human abode, furnished with some elegance.
But few people have the taste to discern, that the art of
embellishing consists in interesting, not in astonishing.

*

Anthony Trollope
The Small House at Allington (1864)

Round the house there were trim gardens, not very large,
but worthy of much note in that they were so trim—gardens
with broad gravel paths, with one walk running in front of
the house so broad as to to be fitly called a terrace. But this,
though in front of the house, was sufficiently removed from
it to allow of a coach-road running inside it to the front door.
The Dales of Allington had always been gardeners, and their

garden was perhaps more noted in the county that any other of their properties. But outside the garden no pretensions had been made to the grandeur of a domain. The pastures round the house were but pretty fields, in which timber was abundant. There was no deer-park at Allington; and though the Allington woods were well known, they formed no portion of a whole of which the house was a part. They lay away, out of sight, a full mile from the back of the house, but not on that account of less avail for the fitting preservation of foxes.

*

Mary Delany

Letter to her sister, 1734 from *The Autobiography and Correspondence of Mary Granville, Mrs. Delany* (1861)

You think, madam, that I have no garden, perhaps? but that's a mistake; I *have one* as big as your parlour in Gloucester, and in it groweth *damask-roses, stocks* variegated and plain, some purple, some red, *pinks, Philaria*, some dead some alive; and *honeysuckles* that never blow.

*

Somerset Maugham

The Magician (1908)

Arthur Burdon and Dr Porhoët walked in silence. They had lunched at a restaurant in the Boulevard Saint Michel, and were sauntering now in the gardens of the Luxembourg. Dr Porhoët walked with stooping shoulders, his hands behind him. He beheld the scene with the eyes of the many painters who have sought by means of the most charming garden in Paris to express their sense of beauty. The grass was scattered with fallen leaves, but their wan decay little served to give a touch of nature to the artifice of all besides. The trees were neatly surrounded by bushes, and the bushes by trim beds of flowers. But the trees grew without abandonment, as though conscious of the decorative scheme they helped to form. It was autumn, and some were leafless already. Many of the flowers were withered. The formal gardens reminded one of a light woman, no longer young, who sought, with faded finery, with powder and paint, to make a brave show of despair. It had those false, difficult smiles of uneasy gaiety, and the pitiful graces which attempt a fascination that the hurrying years have rendered vain.

*

Anton Chekhov
A Dreary Story (1889)

Here is our garden…I fancy it has grown neither better nor worse since I was a student. I don't like it. It would be far more sensible if there were tall pines and fine oaks growing here instead of sickly-looking lime-trees, yellow acacias, and skimpy pollard lilacs. The student whose state of mind is in the majority of cases created by his surroundings, ought in the place where he is studying to see facing him at every turn what is lofty, strong and elegant…God preserve him from gaunt trees, broken windows, grey walls, and doors covered with torn American leather!

*

Jerome K. Jerome
Three Men in a Boat (1889)

Harris asked me if I'd ever been in the maze at Hampton Court. He said he went in once to show somebody else the way. He had studied it up in a map, and it was so simple that it seemed foolish — hardly worth the twopence charged for admission. Harris said he thought that map must have been got up as a practical joke, because it wasn't a bit like the real thing, and only misleading. It was a country cousin that Harris took in. He said:

'We'll just go in here, so that you can say you've been, but it's very simple. It's absurd to call it a maze. You keep on taking the first turning to the right. We'll just walk round for ten minutes, and then go and get some lunch.'

They met some people soon after they had got inside, who said they had been there for three-quarters of an hour, and had had about enough of it. Harris told them they could follow him, if they liked; he was just going in, and then should turn round and come out again. They said it was very kind of him, and fell behind, and followed.

They picked up various other people who wanted to get it over, as they went along, until they had absorbed all the persons in the maze. People who had given up all hopes of ever getting either in or out, or of ever seeing their home and friends again, plucked up courage at the sight of Harris and his party, and joined the procession, blessing him. Harris said he should judge there must have been twenty people, following him, in all; and one woman with a baby, who had been there all the morning, insisted on taking his arm, for fear of losing him.

Harris kept on turning to the right, but it seemed a long way, and his cousin said he supposed it was a very big maze.

'Oh, one of the largest in Europe,' said Harris.

'Yes, it must be,' replied the cousin, 'because we've walked a good two miles already.'

Harris began to think it rather strange himself, but he held on until, at last, they passed the half of a penny bun on the ground that Harris's cousin swore he had noticed there seven minutes ago. Harris said: 'Oh, impossible!' but the woman with the baby said, 'Not at all,' as she herself had taken it from the child, and thrown it down there, just before she met Harris. She also added that she wished she never had met Harris, and expressed an opinion that he was an impostor. That made Harris mad, and he produced his map, and explained his theory.

'The map may be all right enough,' said one of the party, 'if you know whereabouts in it we are now.'

Harris didn't know, and suggested that the best thing to do would be to go back to the entrance, and begin again. For the beginning again part of it there was not much enthusiasm; but with regard to the advisability of going back to the entrance there was complete unanimity, and so they turned, and trailed after Harris again, in the opposite direction. About ten minutes more passed, and then they found themselves in the centre.

Harris thought at first of pretending that that was what he had been aiming at; but the crowd looked dangerous, and he decided to treat it as an accident.

Anyhow, they had got something to start from then. They did know where they were, and the map was once more consulted, and the thing seemed simpler than ever, and off they started for the third time.

And three minutes later they were back in the centre again.

After that, they simply couldn't get anywhere else. Whatever way they turned brought them back to the middle. It became so regular at length, that some of the people stopped there, and waited for the others to take a walk round, and come back to them. Harris drew out his map again, after a while, but the sight of it only infuriated the mob, and they told him to go and curl his hair with it. Harris said that he couldn't help feeling that, to a certain extent, he had become unpopular.

They all got crazy at last, and sang out for the keeper, and the man came and climbed up the ladder outside, and shouted out directions to them. But all their heads were, by this time, in such a confused whirl that they were incapable of grasping anything, and so the man told them to stop where they were, and he would come to them. They huddled together, and waited; and he climbed down, and came in.

He was a young keeper, as luck would have it, and new to the business; and when he got in, he couldn't find them, and he wandered about, trying to get to them, and then *he* got lost. They caught sight of him, every now and then, rushing about the other side of the hedge, and he would see them, and rush to get to them, and they would wait there for about five minutes, and then he would reappear again in exactly the same spot, and ask them where they had been.

They had to wait till one of the old keepers came back from his dinner before they got out.

Harris said he thought it was a very fine maze, so far as he was a judge; and we agreed that we would try to get George to go into it, on our way back.

*

William Trevor
Elizabeth Alone (1973)

He oiled the lawnmower and then turned it upside down. He spun the blades and, less easily, the rollers. The blades needed sharpening, he noticed, but otherwise it really didn't seem a bad machine, and he began to think that maybe two pounds hadn't been excessive after all. That was the trouble with D'arcy and Carstairs: they were never prepared to spend a little time over a matter like that, getting something going by patiently poking at it, like he'd so often got the Zephyr going. It probably wouldn't even have occurred to them that someone quite near at hand might have a secondhand machine lying about; they'd probably have gone off and bought a new one somewhere, The first time he'd driven up to the King of England in the Zephyr they'd both said they were surprised he'd bought it.

Unlike the Zephyr, however, the Passes' lawnmower refused to perform the task for which it had been designed and built twenty-five years ago. This was not wholly the lawnmower's fault. The soil was sodden and the grass was thick and long. The blades succeeded in pulling some of it out by the roots, and long green strings again wound themselves around the axles, preventing them from turning. The man whose lawnmower Henry had tried to borrow in the first place looked over the garden fence and said that a scythe was necessary for the job Henry was attempting. 'One of those rotary things might do it,' the man said, 'when the ground's dried out.' It was unusual, he added, to attempt to cut grass in early February, or to cut grass at any time of the year with the kind of antiquated contraption that Henry had. He then spoke about weeds, saying that when weeds got going in a garden their seeds blew into other people's gardens, causing bad feeling. 'I often wondered if you were aware of that,' the man said, nodding at Henry and going away.

Henry abandoned the grass, resolving to make inquiries in the King of England about how to cut grass in February, when the ground was sodden. He turned his attention to the weeds, and for two and a half hours pulled up dandelion roots and convolvulus, nettles, ragwort, Scotch grass, chickweed, and docks. He dug them out of the soil with a fork, digging up peony tubers and iris tubers as well, and the remains of rose-bushes. He rooted up the Michaelmas daisies that his ex-wife had planted, and chrysanthemums and aubretia. In the house he found the plastic sacks that the mushroom fibre had come in. He filled them with what he'd removed and threw them on to the heap at the bottom of the garden. He forked through the beds he'd cleared, and gathered up bay leaves that had been lying on the ground for some years, refusing to disintegrate. He found a number of empty yoghurt cartons, bottles, tins, and a coat that he must have left in the garden and forgotten about....

At half-past five he'd cleared the front garden to his satisfaction. He found a saw in a coal-bunker at the back of the house and sawed off most of the ash tree. He carried the carton, now overflowing with weeds and trimmings from the tree, though the house to the bottom of the back garden. Spring or something like it seemed to freshen the evening air. A month ago it would have been pitch dark now. The palms of his hands burned with nettle-stings, thorns had torn his flesh, but his mood was buoyant. If he met Mrs Passes he would good-humouredly say that when he'd tried the

mower out it had proved incapable of cutting grass. He'd
laugh and say it didn't matter...

STYLES

There is an extraordinary linkage between the *style* of a garden and the way writers approach it. The unadorned directness of John Clare describing a country garden—really a peasant garden that delights in wild woodbines or sweetbriars dug out of some hedge—is strikingly different from the stately prose of Inigo Thomas and Reginald Blomfield talking about the old formal garden of the seventeenth century. Oddly enough, both styles of garden are praised for their 'simplicity', a word unlikely to be used by Sir George Sitwell in his paean to Villa d'Este's 'umbrageous ilexes' and 'enchanted pools'. There, in the splendour of the high Renaissance, all is complexity and evocation.

But there are many styles of gardens, just as there are many kinds of writers. Those of us who grew up in the American

Midwest will recognize the yearning that drove Willa Cather's Professor to build a French garden, replete with precise hedges and gravel instead of grass, in a university town on the edge of Lake Michigan. Washington Irving's profound admiration for 'landscape gardening' in *The Sketch Book* is confirmed by his own attempts to create a grand estate in Connecticut, while the specialist garden devoted to one variety of plant emerges vividly from Alexandre Dumas' historical tale *The Black Tulip*. For sheer comfort, however, the style of garden most loved by many writers, particularly in the nineteenth century, must be the cottage garden—vegetables, flowers, fruit trees and bushes. See Flora Thompson's *Lark Rise to Candleford* or George Eliot's *Scenes from Clerical Life* for the full flavour.

Reginald Blomfield and Inigo Thomas
The Formal Garden in England (1901)

The characteristic of the old formal garden, the garden of Markham and Lawson, was its exceeding simplicity.

The primary purpose of a garden as a place of retirement and seclusion, a place for quiet thought and leisurely enjoyment, was kept steadily in view. The grass and the yew trees were trimmed close to gain their full beauty from the sunlight.

Sweet kindly flowers filled the knots and borders. Peacocks and pigeons brightened the terraces and lawns. The paths were straight and ample, the garden-house solidly built and comfortable; everything was reasonable and unaffected. But this simple delight in nature and art became feebler as the seventeeth century grew older.

Gardening became the fashionable art, and this was the golden age for professional gardeners; but the real pleasure of it was gone. Rows of statues were introduced from the French, costly architecture superseded the simple terrace, intricate parterres were laid out from gardeners' pattern-books, and meanwhile the flowers were forgotten. It was well that all this pomp should be swept away. We do not want this extravagant statuary, these absurdities in clipped work, this aggressive prodigality. But though one would admit that in its decay the formal garden became unmanageable and absurd, the abuse is no argument against the use. An attempt has been made in this book to show the essential reasonableness of the principles of Formal Gardening, and the sanity of its method when properly handled. The long yew hedge is clipped and shorn because we want its firm boundary lines and the plain mass of its colour; the grass bank is formed into a definite slope to attain the beauty of close-shaven turf at varied angles with the light. The broad grass walk, with its paved footpath at the centre, is cool to walk upon in summer and dry on the pavement in the winter; and the flower border on either side is planted with every kind of delightful flower, so that the refinements of its colour may be enjoyed all through the summer.

*

George Eliot
Scenes from Clerical Life (1858)

The garden was one of those old-fashioned paradises which hardly exist any longer except as memories of our childhood; no finical separation between flower and kitchen-garden there; no monotony of enjoyment for one sense to the exclusion of a another; but a charming, paradisiacal mingling of all that was pleasant to the eye and good for food. The rich flower-border running along every walk, with its endless succession of spring flowers, anemones, auriculas, wall-flowers, sweet-williams, campanulas, snap-dragons, and tiger-lilies, had its taller beauties such as moss and Provence roses, varied with espalier apple-trees; the crimson of a carnation was carried out in the lurking crimson of the neighbouring strawberry beds; you gathered a moss-rose one moment and a bunch of currants the next; you were in a delicious fluctuation between the scent of jasmine and the juice of gooseberries. Then what a high wall at one end, flanked by a summer-house so lofty, that after ascending its long flight of steps you could see perfectly well that there was no view worth looking at; what alcoves and garden-seats in all directions; and along one side, what a hedge, tall, firm and unbroken like a green wall!

*

William Maxwell
The Chateau (1961)

They noticed a gap in the hedge, and, walking through it, found themselves in a huge garden where fruit trees, rose trees, flowers, and vegetables were mingled in a way that surprised and delighted them. So did the scarecrow, which was dressed in striped morning trousers and a blue cotton smock. Under the straw hat the stuffed head had sly features painted on it. They saw old Mme Bonenfant at the far end of the garden, and walked slowly toward her. By the time they arrived at the sweet-pea trench her basket was full. She laid her garden shears across the long green stems and took the Americans on a tour of the garden, pointing out the espaliered fruit trees and telling them the French names of flowers. She did not understand their schoolroom French. They felt shy with her. But the tour did not last very long, and they understood that she was being kind, that she wanted them to feel at home. Leading them to some big fat bushes that were swathed in burlap against the birds, she told them to help themselves to the currants and gooseberries, and then she went down the garden path to the house.

*

Alexandre Dumas
The Black Tulip (1850)

At the time when Cornelius van Baerle began to devote himself to tulip-growing, expending on this hobby his yearly revenue and the guilders of his father, there was at Dort, living next door to him, a citizen of the name of Isaac Boxtel who from the age when he was able to think for himself had indulged the same fancy, and who was in ecstasies at the mere mention of the word "tulban," which (as we are assured by the "Floriste Francaise," the most highly considered authority in matters relating to this flower) is the first word in the Cingalese tongue which was ever used to designate that masterpiece of floriculture which is now called the tulip.

Boxtel had not the good fortune of being rich, like Van Baerle. He had therefore, with great care and patience, and by dint of strenuous exertions, laid out near his house at Dort a garden fit for the culture of his cherished flower; he had mixed the soil according to the most approved prescriptions, and given to his hotbeds just as much heat and fresh air as the strictest rules of horticulture exact.

Isaac knew the temperature of his frames to the twentieth part of a degree. He knew the strength of the current of air, and tempered it so as to adapt it to the wave of the stems of his flowers. His productions also began to meet with the favour of the public. They were beautiful, nay, distinguished. Several fanciers had come to see Boxtel's tulips. At last he had even started amongst all the Linnaeuses and Tourneforts a tulip which bore his name, and which, after having travelled all through France, had found its way into Spain, and penetrated as far as Portugal; and the King, Don Alfonso

VI.—who, being expelled from Lisbon, had retired to the island of Terceira, where he amused himself, not, like the great Conde, with watering his carnations, but with growing tulips—had, on seeing the Boxtel tulip, exclaimed, "Not so bad, by any means!"

All at once, Cornelius van Baerle, who, after all his learned pursuits, had been seized with the tulipomania, made some changes in his house at Dort, which, as we have stated, was next door to that of Boxtel. He raised a certain building in his court-yard by a story, which shutting out the sun, took half a degree of warmth from Boxtel's garden, and, on the other hand, added half a degree of cold in winter; not to mention that it cut the wind, and disturbed all the horticultural calculations and arrangements of his neighbour.

After all, this mishap appeared to Boxtel of no great consequence. Van Baerle was but a painter, a sort of fool who tried to reproduce and disfigure on canvas the wonders of nature. The painter, he thought, had raised his studio by a story to get better light, and thus far he had only been in the right. Mynheer van Baerle was a painter, as Mynheer Boxtel was a tulip-grower; he wanted somewhat more sun for his paintings, and he took half a degree from his neighbour's tulips.

The law was for Van Baerle, and Boxtel had to abide by it.

Besides, Isaac had made the discovery that too much sun was injurious to tulips, and that this flower grew quicker, and had a better colouring, with the temperate warmth of morning, than with the powerful heat of the midday sun. He therefore felt almost grateful to Cornelius van Baerle for having given him a screen gratis.

Maybe this was not quite in accordance with the true state of things in general, and of Isaac Boxtel's feelings in particular. It is certainly astonishing what rich comfort great minds, in the midst of momentous catastrophes, will derive from the consolations of philosophy.

But alas! What was the agony of the unfortunate Boxtel on seeing the windows of the new story set out with bulbs and seedlings of tulips for the border, and tulips in pots; in short, with everything pertaining to the pursuits of a tulip-monomaniac!

There were bundles of labels, cupboards, and drawers with compartments, and wire guards for the cupboards, to allow free access to the air whilst keeping out slugs, mice, dormice, and rats, all of them very curious fanciers of tulips at two thousand francs a bulb.

Boxtel was quite amazed when he saw all this apparatus, but he was not as yet aware of the full extent of his misfortune. Van Baerle was known to be fond of everything that pleases the eye. He studied Nature in all her aspects for the benefit of his paintings, which were as minutely finished as those of Gerard Dow, his master, and of Mieris, his friend. Was it not possible, that, having to paint the interior of a tulip-grower's, he had collected in his new studio all the accessories of decoration?

Yet, although thus consoling himself with illusory suppositions, Boxtel was not able to resist the burning curiosity which was devouring him. In the evening, therefore, he placed a ladder against the partition wall between their gardens, and, looking into that of his neighbour Van Baerle, he convinced himself that the soil of a large square bed, which had formerly been occupied by different plants, was removed, and the ground disposed in beds of loam mixed with river mud (a combination which is particularly favourable to the tulip), and the whole surrounded by a border of turf to keep the soil in its place. Besides this, sufficient shade to temper the noonday heat; aspect south-southwest; water in abundant supply, and at hand; in short, every requirement to insure not only success but also progress. There could not be a doubt that Van Baerle had become a tulip-grower.

Boxtel at once pictured to himself this learned man, with a capital of four hundred thousand and a yearly income of ten thousand guilders, devoting all his intellectual and financial resources to the cultivation of the tulip. He foresaw his neighbour's success, and he felt such a pang at the mere idea of this success that his hands dropped powerless, his knees trembled, and he fell in despair from the ladder.

And thus it was not for the sake of painted tulips, but for real ones, that Van Baerle took from him half a degree of warmth. And thus Van Baerle was to have the most admirably fitted aspect, and, besides, a large, airy, and well ventilated chamber where to preserve his bulbs and seedlings; while he, Boxtel, had been obliged to give up for this purpose his bedroom, and, lest his sleeping in the same apartment might injure his bulbs and seedlings, had taken up his abode in a miserable garret.

*

Joseph Conrad
Nostromo (1904)

After lunch, Doña Emilia and the señor doctor came slowly through the inner gateway of the patio. The large gardens of the Casa Gould, surrounded by high walls, and the red-tile slopes of neighbouring roofs, lay open before them, with masses of shade under the trees and level surfaces of sunlight upon the lawns. A triple row of old orange trees surrounded the whole. Barefooted, brown gardeners, in snowy white shirts and wide *calzoneras*, dotted the grounds, squatting over flowerbeds, passing between the trees, dragging slender India-rubber tubes across the gravel of the paths; and the fine jets of water crossed each other in graceful curves, sparkling in the sunshine with a slight pattering noise upon the bushes, and an effect of showered diamonds upon the grass.

*

Washington Irving
The Sketch Book (1820)

The taste of the English is the cultivation of land, and in what is called landscape gardening, is unrivalled. They have studied nature intently, and discover an exquisite sense of her beautiful forms and harmonious combinations. These charms, which in other countries she lavishes in wild solitudes, are here assembled round the haunts of domestic life. They seem to have caught her coy and furtive graces, and spread them, like witchery, about their rural abodes.

Nothing can be more imposing than the magnificence of

English park scenery. Vast lawns that extend like sheets of vivid green, with here and there clumps of gigantic trees, heaping up rich piles of foliage: the solemn pomp of groves and woodland glades, with the deer trooping in silent herds across them; the hare, bounding away to the covert; or the pheasant, suddenly bursting upon the wing: the brook, taught to wind in natural meanderings or expand into a glassy lake: the sequestered pool, reflecting the quivering trees, with the yellow leaf sleeping on its bosom, and the trout roaming fearlessly about its limpid waters; while some rustic temple or sylvan statue, grown green and dank with age, gives an air of classic sanctity to the seclusion.

*

Sir George Sitwell
An Essay on the Making of Gardens (1909)

... Villa d'Este, where the great heart of the Anio throbs through the garden and every grove and thicket and alley is filled with a tumult of sobbing sound. It is a place of mysterious silence, of low-weeping fountains and muffled footfalls; a garden of sleep. The gates are on a lower level, and athwart the rose-tangled slope to the left the architect has thrown five great slanting staircases of stone, broad enough and splendid enough to carry an army of guests to the plateau above. But this is now a solitude, a mournful ilex *bosco* with cross walks and mossy fountains shaped like the baluster of some great sundial. From the central stairway, not far from the house, a broader opening in the woodland leads to a alwn and pool below the great cascade. In front is a long cliff crowned with ilex forest and faced with a frontispiece of moss-grown arches and bubbling fountains. The main fall drops from a balcony between two tall umbrageous ilexes which rise on either hand like the horns of an Addisonian periwig; from basin to basin it drops in a silver fringe, held in by low serpentine walls that curve and re-curve like the arches of a bridge or the edges of a shell. Through vaults on either hand, long winding stairways follow the curves, the masonry is choked with ferns, the steps with weeds, and riotous water-plants crowd upon the ledges or thrust green juicy stems through the scum which has gathered in the corners of the pools. At the top, in a small irregular clearing walled by wild ilex wood and wilder tangle of flowering shrubs, is a balustraded basin in the form of a great *quatrefoil*. Gold-red fish gleam in the sea-green water, which reflects soft foliage and lichened stone and patches of pearly light; in the centre a huge cylinder of moss supports the silvery feathers of a fountain; it is the enchanted pool in a fairy woodland. But the traveller who has wandered here alone on a drowsy afternoon does not linger to listen to the trickle of the fountain and the murmuring of the bees. From below the threshold of the mind a strange sense of hidden danger oppresses him, an instinct neither to be reasoned with nor to be understood. Can there be brigands yet in the forest heights, or is the place by shades of the soldiers who once fell in battle about the pool? He waits and wrestles with his folly, then sadly descending the slippery stairways leaves cooling fount and shaded alley for the torrid sunshine of the outer world.

It is death to sleep in the garden.

*

John Clare
"Proposals for Building a Cottage" *The Village Minstrel* (1821)

Beside a runnel build my shed,
With stubbles cover'd o'er;
Let broad oaks o'er its chimney spread,
And grass-plats grace the door.

The door may open with a string,
So that it closes tight;
And locks would be a wanted thing,
To keep out thieves at night.

A little garden, not too fine,
Inclose with painted pales;
And woodbines, round the cot to twine,
Pin to the wall with nails.

Let hazels grow, and spindling sedge,
Bend bowering over-head;
Dig old man's beard from woodland hedge,
To twine a summer shade.

Beside the threshold sods provide,
And build a summer seat;
Plant sweet-briar bushes by its side,
And flowers that blossom sweet.

I love the sparrow's ways to watch
Upon the cotter's sheds,
So here and there pull out the thatch,
That they may hide their heads.

And as the sweeping swallows stop
Their flights along the green,
Leave holes within the chimney-top
To paste their nest between.

Stick shelves and cupboards round the hut,
In all the holes and nooks;
Nor in the corner fail to put
A cupboard for the books.

Along the floor some sand I'll sift,
To make it fit to live in;
And then I'll thank ye for the gift,
As something worth the giving.

*

Willa Cather

The Professor's House (1925)

From one of the dismantled windows the Professor happened
to look out into his back garden, and at that cheerful sight he
went quickly downstairs and escaped from the dusty air and
brutal light of the empty rooms.

His walled-in garden had been the comfort of his life—
and it was the one thing his neighbours held against him. He
started to make it soon after the birth of his first daughter,

when his wife began to be unreasonable about his spending so much time at the lake and on the tennis court. In this undertaking he got help and encouragement from his landlord, a retired German farmer, good-natured and lenient about everything but spending money. If the Professor happened to have a new baby at home, or a faculty dinner, or an illness in the family, or any unusual expense, Appelhoff cheerfully waited for the rent, but pay for repairs he would not. When it was a question of the garden, however, the old man sometimes stretched a point. He helped his tenant with seeds and slips and sound advice, and with his twisted old back. He even spent a little money to bear half the expense of the stucco wall.

The Professor had succeeded in making a French garden in Hamilton. There was not a blade of grass; it was a tidy half-acre of glistening gravel and glistening shrubs and bright flowers. There were trees, of course; a spreading horse-chestnut, a row of slender Lombardy poplars at the back, along the white wall, and in the middle two symmetrical, round-topped linden trees. Masses of green-brier grew in the corners, the prickly stems interwoven and clipped until they were like great bushes. There was a bed for salad herbs. Salmon-pink geraniums dripped over the wall. The French marigolds and dahlias were just now at their best—such dahlias as no one else in Hamilton could grow. St. Peter had tended this bit of ground for over twenty years, and had got the upper hand of it. In the spring, when home-sickness and the fret of things unaccomplished awoke, he worked off his discontent here. In the long hot summers, when he could not go abroad, he stayed at home with his garden, sending his wife and daughters to Colorado to escape the humid prairie heat, so nourishing to wheat and corn, so exhausting to human beings. In these months when he was a bachelor again, he brought down his books and papers and worked in a desk chair under the linden-trees; breakfasted and lunched and had his tea in the garden. And it was here that he and Tom Outland used to sit and talk half through the warm, soft nights.

*

Flora Thompson
Lark Rise to Candleford (1939)

Narrow paths between high, built-up banks supporting flower borders, crowded with jonquils, auriculas, forget-me-nots and other spring flowers, led from one part of the garden to another. One winding path led down the earth closet in its bower of nut-trees halfway down the garden, another to the vegetable garden and on to the rough grass plot before the beehives. Between each section were thick groves of bushes with ferns and capers and Solomon's seal, so closed in that the long, rough grass there was always damp. Wasted ground, a good gardener might have said, but delightful in its cool, green shadiness.

Nearer the house was a portion entirely given up to flowers, not growing in beds or borders, but crammed together in an irregular square, where they bloomed in half-wild profusion. There were rose bushes there and lavender and rosemary and a bush apple-tree that bore little red and yellow streaked apples in later summer, and Michaelmas daisies and red-hot pokers and old-fashioned pompom dahlias in autumn and peonies and pinks already budding.

An old man in the village came one day a week to till the vegetable garden, but the flower garden was no one's especial business. Miss Lane herself would occasionally pull on a pair of wash-leather gloves and transplant a few seedlings; Matthew would pull up a weed or stake a plant as he passed, and the smiths, once a year, turned out of the shop to dig between the roots and cut down dead canes. Between whiles the flowers grew just as they would in crowded masses, perfect in their imperfection.

SINISTER

Gardens in fiction are not necessarily delightful. On the contrary, some can evoke very much the opposite impression. Dr. Johnson finds 'horrible profundity' at Hawkstone Park. A garden may suggest, as in Charlotte Brontë's *Villette,* the malign presence of a ghost, or simply through an oppressive atmosphere—as in *The Plumed Serpent* by D. H. Lawrence—a sense of death or lethargy. In Lawrence's case, even scents, 'moving thick and noiseless', contribute to the effect, while in *The Leopard* by Giuseppe Tomasi de Lampedusa it is only the 'cloying, fleshy and slightly putrid' odours that redeem the garden at all: 'It was a garden for the blind: a constant offense to the eyes, a pleasure strong if somewhat crude to the nose'.

Probably the most famous of all sinister gardens is that belonging to Dr. Rappaccini in Nathaniel Hawthorne's ghoulish story "Rappaccini's Daughter". Here the flowers and shrubs have been deliberately chosen for their poisonous qualities. Horror is not merely implied, but inevitable. However magnificent the plantings may be, they speak ultimately of nothing but death.

Charlotte Brontë
Villette (1853)

Behind the house at the Rue Fossette there was a garden—
large, considering that it lay in the heart of a city, and to
my recollection at this day it seems pleasant: but time, like
distance, lends to certain scenes an influence so softening;
and where all is stone around, blank wall and hot pavement,
how precious seems one shrub, how lovely an enclosed and
planted spot of ground!

There went a tradition that Madame Beck's house had in
old days been a convent. That in years gone by—how long
gone by I cannot tell, but I think some centuries—before the
city had over-spread this quarter, and when it was tilled ground
and avenue, and such deep and leafy seclusion as ought to
embosom a religious house—that something had happened
on this site which, rousing fear and inflicting horror, had left
to the place the inheritance of a ghost-story. A vague tale
went of a black and white nun, sometimes, on some night
or nights of the year, seen in some part of this vicinage. The
ghost must have been built out some ages ago, for there were
houses all round now; but certain convent-relics, in the shape
of old and huge fruit trees, yet consecrated the spot; and, at
the foot of one—a Methuselah of a pear-tree, dead, all but
a few boughs which still faithfully renewed their perfumed
snow in spring, and their honey-sweet pendants in autumn—
you saw, scraping away the mossy earth between the half-
bared roots, a glimpse of a slab, smooth, hard, and black.
The legend went, unconfirmed and unaccredited, but still
propagated, that this was the portal of a vault, imprisoning
deep beneath that ground, on whose surface grass grew

and flowers bloomed, the bones of a girl whom a monkish conclave of the drear middle ages had here buried alive for some sin against her vow. Her shadow it was that tremblers had feared, through long generations after her poor frame was dust; her black robe and white veil that, for timid eyes, moonlight and shade had mocked, as they fluctuated in the night-wind through the garden-thicket.

Independently of romantic rubbish, however, that old garden had its charms. On summer mornings I used to rise early, to enjoy them alone; on summer evenings, to linger solitary, to keep tryste with the rising moon, or taste one kiss of the evening breeze, or fancy rather than feel the freshness of dew descending. The turf was verdant, the gravelled walks were white; sun-bright nasturtiums clustered beautiful about the roots of the doddered orchard giants. There was a large berceau, above which spread the shade of an acacia; there was a smaller, more sequestered bower, nestled in the vines which ran all along a high and grey wall, and gathered their tendrils in a knot of beauty, and hung their clusters in loving profusion about the favoured spot where jasmine and ivy met and married them.

*

Robert Harbison
Eccentric Spaces (1977)

Bomarzo in its present state will not fit many people's notion of a garden. Perhaps the easiest thing to call it is a fantastic landscape left purposely and glaringly incomplete, lacking consistency or inevitability except that all the stone nightmares occurred to the same dreamer, loosely strung variations on an obsession. The project...is a collection of grotesque garden follies, many carved in natural outcroppings and hence located irregularly in a small piece of bumpy woodland near the little hillside town of Bomarzo. They can never have been visited by many people in this wild place, made more wild by Orsini's imaginings, but the rock is nonetheless covered with explanatory, justificatory, admonitory inscriptions. The garden is a powerful monologue and brings home poignantly that gardens never just *are* like landscapes, but need to be responded to, making our admiration feel human because it amounts to paying someone a compliment.

The odd tilt of Orsini's mind is evident in the first structure he had built, for which he employed a famous architect. Vignola's circular pavilion has an ample and graceful rectangular porch but no door gives on the temple from it, that is found on the other side. Already Orsini invites and then rebuffs, begins civil but is seized by a bearish whim, a tangle of motives which becomes more acute in the other enterable structures on the grounds. One of them is a howling face ten or twelve feet high whose mouth opens to make a little chamber lit by his dark eyes. A tongue floats in the gloom which turns out to be a delicately fashioned table for picnic surrounded by benches of teeth. Grotesque faces are familiar ones in the designs of the period, one of its ornamental clichés, but here by overheated enlargement Orsini permanently acts cannibal aggression. What can be quaffed at this table but the black juices of hatred? And yet he spells it out, says 'Tremble, Marvel', as if the terror will wear off.

Orsini's park of monsters is a determined effort to make a mood eternal, to memorialize an intense disgust. Finally what is astonishing is not the physical presence but the guessed intention, the desire to preserve bitter and fugitive sensations. We find some appropriateness in the way he has done it—the amateur carvers are more effective than masters in conveying the rough impatience of the sentiment; the creatures springing or half sprung from the rocks seem crystallizations of the foul air—but we only know how we are to feel without feeling it. In the end his torment is inaccessible, he communicates the fact of it in an imagery relentlessly strange yet inevitably borrowed, and, this man who parades his unending distresses remains remote. Some of this failure is in the mixture of his purposes—he cries for help yet he wants to wound, to show that a didactic unsociable art is impossible, and ministers to our suspicions of Italian self-display at any price.

*

D. H. Lawrence
The Plumed Serpent (1926)

The square, inner patio, dark, with sun lying on the heavy arches of one side, had pots of red and white flowers, but was ponderous, as if dead for centuries. A certain dead, heavy strength and beauty seemed there, unable to pass away, unable to liberate itself and decompose. There was a stone basin of clear but motionless water, and the heavy red-and-yellow arches went round the courtyard with warrior-like fatality, their bases in dark shadow. Dead, massive house of the Conquistadores, with a glimpse of tall-grown garden beyond, and further Aztec cypresses rising to strange dark heights. And dead silence, like the black, porous, absorptive lava rock. Save when the tram-cars battered past the outside solid wall.

—

In the archway downstairs, Don Ramón and the General took their leave. The rest trailed on into the garden.

Evening was falling. The garden was drawn up tall, under the huge dark trees on the one side and the tall, reddish-and-yellow house on the other. It was like being at the bottom of some dusky, flowering garden down in Hades. Hibicus hung scarlet from the bushes, putting out yellow bristling tongues. Some roses were scattering scentless petals on the twilight, and lonely-looking carnations hung on weak stalks. From a huge dense bush the mysterious white bells of the datura were suspended, large and silent, like the very ghosts of sound. And the datura scent was moving thick and noiseless from the tree, into the little alleys.

*

Samuel Johnson
On Hawkstone Park, seat of Sir Rowland Hill (1774)

By the extent of its prospects, the awfulness of its shades, the horrors of its precipices, the verdure of its hollows, and the loftiness of its rocks, the ideas which it forces upon the mind are the sublime, the dreadful, and the vast. Above, is inaccessible altitude, below is horrible profundity.

*

Nikolai Gogol
Dead Souls (1842)

Not many people would have admired the situation of Manilov's abode, for it stood on an isolated rise and was open to every wind that blew. On the slope of the rise lay closely-mown turf, while, disposed here and there, after the English fashion, were flower-beds containing clumps of lilac and yellow acacia. Also, there were a few insignificant groups of slender-leaved, pointed-tipped birch trees, with, under two of the latter, an arbour having a shabby green cupola, some blue-painted wooden supports, and the inscription "This is the Temple of Solitary Thought." Lower down the slope lay a green-coated pond—green-coated ponds constitute a frequent spectacle in the gardens of Russian landowners; and, lastly, from the foot of the declivity there stretched a line of mouldy, log-built huts which, for some obscure reason or another, our hero set himself to count. Up to two hundred or more did he count, but nowhere could he perceive a single leaf of vegetation or a single stick of timber. The only thing to greet the eye was the logs of which the huts were constructed.

*

Giuseppe Tomasi di Lampedusa
The Leopard
Translated by Archibald Colquhoun (1958)

With a wildly excited Bendicò bounding ahead of him he went down the short flight of steps into the garden. Enclosed between three walls and the side of the house, its seclusion gave it the air of a cemetery, accentuated by the parallel little mounds bounding the irrigation canals and looking like the graves of very tall, very thin giants. Plants were growing in thick disorder on the the reddish clay; flowers sprouted in all directions; and the myrtle hedges seemed put there to prevent movement rather than guide it. At the end a statue of Flora with yellow-black lichen exhibited her centuries-old charms with an air of resignation; on each side were benches holding quilted cushions, also of grey marble; and in a corner the gold of an acacia tree introduced a sudden note of gaiety. Every sod seemed to exude a yearning for beauty soon muted by languor.

But the garden, hemmed in and almost squashed between these barriers, was exhaling scents that were cloying, fleshy and slightly putrid, like to aromatic liquids distilled from the relics of certain saints; the carnations superimposed their pungence on the formal fragrance of roses and the oily emanations of magnolias drooping in corners; and somewhere beneath it all was a faint smell of mint mingling with a nursery whiff of acacia and a jammy one of myrtle; from a grove beyond the wall came an erotic waft of early orange-blossom.

It was a garden for the blind: a constant offense to the eyes, a pleasure strong if somewhat crude to the nose. The *Paul Neyron* rose, whose cuttings he had himself bought in Paris, had degenerated; first stimulated and then enfeebled by the strong if languid pull of Sicilian earth, burnt by apocalyptic Julys, they had changed into objects like flesh-coloured cabbages, obscene and distilling a dense almost incandescent scent which no French horticulturist would have dared hope for. The Prince put one under his nose and seemed to be sniffing the thigh of a dancer from the Opera.

Bendicò, to whom it was also proffered, drew back in disgust and hurried off in search of healthier sensations amid dead lizards and manure.

*

Nathaniel Hawthorne
"Rappaccini's Daughter" from *Mosses from an Old Manse and Other Stories* (1853)

Giovanni still found no better occupation than to look down into the garden beneath his window. From its appearance, he judged it to be one of those botanic gardens which were of earlier date in Padua than elsewhere in Italy or in the world. Or, not improbably, it might once have been a pleasure-place of an opulent family, for there was the ruin of a marble fountain in the centre, sculptured with rare art, but so wofully shattered that it was impossible to trace the original design from the chaos of remaining fragments. The water, however, continued to gush and sparkle into the sunbeams as cheerfully as ever. A little gurgling sound ascended to the young man's window, and made him feel as if the fountain were an immortal spirit that sang its song unceasingly and without heeding the vicissitudes around it, while one century embodied it in marble and another scattered the perishable garniture on the soil. All about the pool into which the water subsided grew various plants, that seemed to require a plentiful supply of moisture for the nourishment of gigantic leaves, and in some instances, flowers gorgeously magnificent. There was one shrub in particular, set in a marble vase in the midst of the pool, that bore a profusion of purple blossoms, each of which had the lustre and richness of a gem; and the whole together made a show so resplendent that it seemed enough to illuminate the garden, even had there been no sunshine. Every portion of the soil was peopled with plants and herbs, which, if less beautiful, still bore tokens of assiduous care, as if all had their individual virtues, known to the scientific mind that fostered them. Some were placed in urns, rich with old carving, and others in common garden pots; some crept serpent-like along the ground or climbed on high, using whatever means of ascent was offered them. One plant had wreathed itself round a statue of Vertumnus, which was then quite veiled and shrouded in a drapery of hanging foliage, so happily arranged that it might have served a sculptor for a study.

While Giovanni stood at the window he heard a rustling behind a screen of leaves, and became aware that a person was at work in the garden. His tall figure soon emerged into view, and showed itself to be that of no common laborer, but a tall, emaciated, sallow, and sickly-looking man, dressed in a scholar's garb of black. He was beyond the middle term of life, with gray hair, a thin, gray beard, and a face singularly marked with intellect and cultivation but could never, even in his more youthful days, have expressed much warmth of heart.

Nothing could exceed the intentness with which this scientific gardener examined every shrub that grew in his path: it seemed as if he was looking in their inmost nature, making observations in regard to their creative essence, and discovering why one leaf grew in this shape and another in that, and wherefore such and such flowers differed among themselves in hue and perfume. Nevertheless, in spite of this deep intelligence on his part, there was no approach to intimacy between himself and these vegetable existences. On the contrary, he avoided their actual touch or the direct inhaling of their odors with a caution that impressed Giovanni most disagreeably; for the man's demeanor was that of one walking among malignant influences, such as savage beasts, or deadly snakes, or evil spirits, which, should he allow them one moment of license, would wreak upon him some terrible fatality. It was strangely frightful to the young man's imagination to see this air of insecurity` in a person cultivating a garden, that most simple and innocent of human toils, and which had been alike the joy and labor of the unfallen parents of the race. Was this garden, then, the Eden of the present world? And this man, with such perception of harm in what his own hands caused to grow,—was he the Adam?

*

Ivan Turgenev

"Phantoms" from *Dream Tales and Prose Poems* (1878)

Again a veil fell over my eyes...Again I lost consciousness. The veil was withdrawn at last. What was it down there below? What was this park, with avenues of lopped lime-trees, with isolated fir-trees of the shape of parasols, with porticoes and temples in the Pompadour style, with statues of satyrs and nymphs of the Bernini school, with rococo tritons in the midst of meandering lakes, closed in by low parapets of blackened marble? Wasn't it Versailles? No, it was not Versailles. A small palace, also rococo, peeped out behind a clump of bushy oaks. The moon shone dimly, shrouded in mist, and over the earth there was, as it spread out, a delicate smoke.

The eye could not decide what it was, whether moonlight or fog. On one of the lakes a swan was asleep; its long back was white as the snow of the frost-bound steppes, while glow-worms gleamed like diamonds in the bluish shadow at the base of a statue.

'We are near Mannheim,' said Alice; 'this is the Schwetzingen garden.'

*

INTENSITIES

Gardens can affect some writers so deeply that their descriptions approach a transcendent state. It is as if they are overwhelmed by the scents and the colours and fall into a kind of ecstasy. The type example of this phenomenon is Andrew Marvell, lost in botanical happiness as he finds the world reduced to 'a green thought in a green shade', but there are other equally excited passages from writers as different as Elizabeth Gaskell and John Donne. What links these writers is their extreme sensitivity—bared nerves, even—to their surroundings. Given that a garden is the ultimate in deliberately created surroundings, the intensity makes sense.

Yet simply feeling strongly is hardly enough to convey bedazzlement. You also need to be a genius with words. Thus when the American novelist Eudora Welty describes dusk coming to her garden and feels 'without ceasing each change in the garden itself', we are like her, moved. Virginia Woolf conveys a state of near hysteria amid the flowers and foliage of Kew Gardens, and we believe her. And Sei Shōnagon, caught up in watching the morning dew slowly dry in a garden in tenth century Kyoto, presents us with a vision of beauty in tiny things that we won't soon forget. At least I will not.

Eudora Welty
Letter to her agent, 1941

Every evening when the sun is going down and it is cool enough to water the garden, and it is all quiet except for the locusts in great waves of sound, and I stand still in one place for a long time putting water on the plants, I feel something new...as if my will went out of me, as if I had a stubbornness and it was melting...

I feel without ceasing every change in the garden itself, the changes of light as the atmosphere grows darker, and the springing up of a wind, and the rhythm of the locusts, and the colors of certain flowers that become very moving—they all seem to be part of a some happiness or unhappiness, an unhappiness that something is lost or left unknown or undone perhaps—and no longer simple in their own beautiful 'outward' way.

*

Horace Walpole
Letter to George Montagu, June 10, 1765

Eleven at night

I am just come out of the garden in the most oriental of all evenings, and from breathing odours beyond those of Araby. The acacias, which the Arabians have the sense to worship, are covered with blossoms, the honeysuckles dangle from every tree in festoons, the seringas are thickets of sweets, and the new-cut hay in the field tempers the balmy gales with simple freshness; while a thousand sky-rockets launched into the air at Ranelagh or Marybone illuminate the scene, and give it an air of Haroun Alraschid's paradise. I was not quite content by daylight; some foreigners dined here, and, though they admire our verdure, it mortified me by its brownness—we have not had a drop of rain this month to cool the tip of our daisies.

*

Honoré de Balzac
Eugénie Grandet (1834)

Along the low mouldering stone wall there was a fence of open lattice-work rotten with age, and fast falling to pieces; overrun by various creeping plants that clambered over it at their own sweet will. A couple of stunted apple trees spread out their gnarled and twisted branches on either side of the wicket gate that led into the garden—three straight walks with strips of border in between, and a line of box-edging on either side; and, at the further end, underneath the ramparts, a sort of arbour of lime trees, and a row of raspberry canes. A huge Walnut tree grew at the end nearest the house, and almost overshadowed the cooper's strong-room with its spreading branches.

It was one of those soft bright autumn mornings peculiar to the districts along the Loire; there was not a trace of mist; the light frosty rime of the previous night was rapidly disappearing as the mild rays of the autumn sun shone on the picturesque surroundings, the old walls, the green tangled growth in the yard and garden.

All these things had been long familiar to Eugénie's eyes,

but today it seemed to her that there was a new beauty about them. A throng of confused thoughts filled her mind as the sunbeams overflowed the world without. A vague, inexplicable new happiness stirred within her, and enveloped her soul, as a bright cloud might cling about some object in the material world. The quaint garden, the old walls, every detail in her little world seemed to be living through this new experience with her; the nature without her was in harmony with her inmost thoughts. The sunlight crept along the wall till it reached a maidenhair fern; the changing hues of a pigeon's breast shone from the thick fronds and glossy stems, and all Eugénie's future grew bright with radiant hopes. Henceforward the bit of wall, its pale flowers, its blue harebells and bleached grasses, was a pleasant sight for her; it called up associations which had all the charm of memories of childhood.

*

Virginia Woolf
"Kew Gardens" from *Monday or Tuesday* (1921)

From the oval-shaped flower-bed there rose perhaps a hundred stalks spreading into heart-shaped or tongue-shaped leaves half way up and unfurling at the tip red or blue or yellow petals marked with spots of colour raised upon the surface, and from the red, blue or yellow gloom of the throat emerged a straight bar, rough with gold dust and slightly clubbed at the end. The petals were voluminous enough to be stirred by the summer breeze, and when they moved, the red, blue and yellow lights passed one over the other, staining an inch of the brown earth beneath with a spot of the most intricate colour...

Thus one couple after another with much the same irregular and aimless movement passed the flower-bed and were enveloped in layer after layer of green blue vapour, in which at first their bodies had substance and a dash of colour, but later both substance and colour dissolved in the green-blue atmosphere. How hot it was! So hot that even the thrush chose to hop, like a mechanical bird, in the shadow of the flowers, with long pauses between one movement and the next; instead of rambling vaguely the white butterflies danced one above the other, making with their white shifting flakes the outline of a shattered marble column above the tallest flowers; the glass roofs of the palm house shone as if a whole market full of shiny green umbrellas had opened in the sun; and in the drone of the aeroplane the voice of the summer sky murmured its fierce soul. Yellow and black, pink and snow white, shapes of all these colours, men, women and children were spotted for a second upon the horizon, and then, seeing the breath of yellow that lay upon the grass, they wavered and sought shade beneath the trees, dissolving like drops of water in the yellow and green atmosphere, staining it faintly with red and blue. It seemed as if all gross and heavy bodies had sunk down in the heat motionless and lay huddled upon the ground, but their voices went wavering from them as if they were flames lolling from the thick waxen bodies of candles. Voices. Yes, voices. Wordless voices, breaking the silence suddenly with such depths of contentment, such passion of desire, or, in the voices of children, such freshness of surprise; breaking the silence? But there was no silence; all the time the motor omnibuses were turning their wheels

and changing their gears; like a vast nest of Chinese boxes all
of wrought steel turning ceaselessly one within another the
city murmured; on the top of which the voices cried aloud
and the petals of myriads of flowers flashed their colours in
the air.

*

Thom Gunn
"The Garden of the Gods" from *The Garden of
the Gods* (1968)

All plants grow here; the most minute,
Glowing from turf, is in its place.
The constant vision of the race;
Lawned orchard deep with flower and fruit.

So bright, that some who see it near,
Think there is lapis on the stems,
And think green, blue, and crimson gems
Hang from the vines and briars here.

They follow path to path in wonder
Through the intense undazzling light.
Nowhere does blossom flare so white!
Nowhere so black is earthmould under!

It goes, though it may come again.
But if at last they try to tell,
They search for trope or parallel,
And cannot, after all, explain.

Where my foot rests, I hear the creak
From generations of my kin,
Layer on layer, pressed leaf-thin.
They merely are. They cannot speak.

This was the garden's place of birth:
I trace it downward from my mind,
Through breast and calf I feel it vined,
And rooted in the death-rich earth.

*

Sei Shōnagon

The Pillow Book of Sei Shōnagon (circa 1000 AD)

Translated by Ivan Morris

I remember a clear morning in the Ninth Month when it had been raining all night. Despite the bright sun, dew was still dripping from the chrysanthemums in the garden. On the bamboo fences and criss-cross hedges I saw tatters of spider web; and where the threads were broken the raindrops hung on them like strings of white pearls.

As it became sunnier, the dew gradually vanished from the clover and other plants where it had lain so heavily; the branches began to stir, then suddenly sprang up of their own accord. Later I described to people how beautiful it all was. What most impressed me was that they were not at all impressed.

—

On the day after a fierce autumn wind everything moves one deeply. The garden is in a pitiful state with all the bamboo and lattice fences knocked over and lying next to each other on the ground. It is bad enough if the branches of one of the great trees have been broken by the wind; but it is a really painful surprise to find that the tree itself has fallen down and is now lying flat over the bush-clover and the valerians. As one sits in one's room looking out, the wind, as though on purpose, gently blows the leaves one by one through the chinks of the lattice window, and one finds it hard to believe that this is the same wind which yesterday raged so violently....In the garden a group of maids and young girls were collecting the flowers and plants that the wind had torn up by the roots and were propping up some that were less damaged. Several women were gathered in front of me by the blind, and I enjoyed seeing how envious they looked as they watched the young people outside and wished that they might join them.

*

Patrick White
The Eye of the Storm (1973)

The nurse recognized the silence which comes when night has almost exhausted itself; light still barely disentangled from the skeins of mist strung across the park; at the foot of the tiered hill on which the house aspired, a cloud of roses floating in its own right, none of the frost-locked buds from Elizabeth Hunter's dream, but great actual clusters at the climax of their beauty.

After she had rummaged for the shears and the ravelled basket under the pantry sink, Mary de Santis let herself into the garden. A dew was falling, settling on her skin; vertical leaves were running moisture; trumpets of the evening before had furled into crinkled phalluses; grass was wearing a bloom it loses on becoming lawn. Encouraged by the rites of innocent sensuality of which she was invited to take part, she tore off a leaf, sucked it, finally bit it to reach the juicy acerbity inside. Not a single cat appeared to dispute her possession of its spiritual enclave as she rubbed, shamefully joyous, past shaggy bark, through flurries of trickling fronds. If her conscience attempted to restrain her, it was forcibly appeased by the tribute of roses she saw herself offering Elizabeth Hunter.

As soon as arrived, she began to snatch like a hungry goat. Dew sprinkling around her in showers. Thorns gashing. Her heels tottered obliquely when not planted in a compost of leaves and sodden earth. Nothing could be done about the worms, lashing themselves into a frenzy of pink exposure: she was too obsessed by her vice of roses. When she stooped to cut into the stems, more than the perfume, the pointed buds themselves could have been shooting up her greedy nostrils, while blown heads, colliding with her flanks, crumbled away, to lie on the neutral earth in clots of cream, splashes of crimson, gentle heart-shaped rose rose.

Breathing deeply, still automatically snipping by spasms at the air, she regained the grass verge, her basket of spoils heavy on her arm. Poured in steadily increasing draughts through the surrounding trees, the light translated the heap of passive roseflesh back into dew, light, pure colour. It might have saddened her to think her own dichotomy of earthbound flesh and aspiring spirit could never be resolved so logically if footsteps along the pavement had not begun breaking into her trance of roses.

*

John Donne
Twicknam Garden (ca. 1607)

Blasted with sighs, and surrounded with teares,
Hither I come to seeke the spring,
And at mine eyes, and at mine eares,
Receive such balmes, as else cure every thing.
But O, selfe traytor, I do bring
The spider love, which transubstantiates all,
And can convert Manna to gall,
And that this place may thoroughly be thought
  True Paradise, I have the serpent brought.

'Twere wholesomer for mee, that winter did
Benight the glory of this place,
And that a grave frost did forbid
These trees to laugh, and mocke mee to my face;
But that I may not this disgrace
Indure, nor yet leave loving, Love let mee
Some senslesse peece of this place bee;
Make mee a mandrake, so I may groane here,
Or a stone fountaine weeping out my yeare.

Hither with christall vyals, lovers come,
And take my teares, which are loves wine,
And try your mistresse Teares at home,
For all are false, that tast not just like mine;
Alas, hearts do not in eyes shine,
Nor can you more judge womans thoughts by teares,
Then by her shadow, what she weares.
O perverse sexe, where none is true but shee,
Who's therefore true, because her truth kills mee.

*

Elizabeth Gaskell
Wives and Daughters (1864 – 1866)

But she lost all consciousness of herself by and by when
the party strolled out into the beautiful grounds, the like
of which she had never even imagined. Green velvet lawns,
bathed in sunshine, stretched away on every side into the
finely wooded park; it there were divisions and ha-has
between the soft sunny sweeps of grass, and the dark gloom
of the forest-trees beyond, Molly did not see them; and the
melting away of exquisite cultivation into the wilderness had
an inexplicable charm to her. Near the house there were walls
and fences; but they were covered with climbing roses, and
rare honeysuckles and other creepers just bursting into bloom.
There were flower-beds, too, scarlet, crimson, blue, orange;
masses of blossom lying on the greensward. Molly held Miss
Browning's hand very tight as they loitered about in company
with several other ladies, and marshalled by a daughter of the
Towers, who seemed half amused at the voluble admiration

showered down upon every possible thing and place. Molly said nothing, as became her age and position, but every now and then she relieved her full heart by drawing a deep breath, almost like a sigh. Presently they came to the long glittering range of greenhouses and hothouses, and an attendant gardener was there to admit the party. Molly did not care for this half so much as for the flowers in the open air; but Lady Agnes had a more scientific taste, she expiated on the rarity of this plant, and the mode of cultivation required by that, till Molly began to feel very faint. She was too shy to speak for some time; but at length, afraid of making a greater sensation if she began to cry, or if she fell against the stands of precious flowers, she caught at Miss Browning's hand, and gasped out—

'May I go back, out into the garden? I can't breathe here!'

'Oh, yes, to be sure, love. I dare say it's hard understanding for you, love; but it's very fine and instructive, and a deal of Latin in it too.'

She turned hastily round not to lose another word of Lady Agnes's lecture on orchids, and Molly turned back and passed out of the heated atmosphere. She felt better in the fresh air; and unobserved, and at liberty, went from one lovely spot to another, now in the open park, now in some shut-in flower-garden, where the song of the birds, and the drip of the central fountain, were the only sounds, and the tree-tops made an enclosing circle in the blue June sky; she went along without more thought as to her whereabouts than a butterfly has, as it skims from flower to flower, till at length she grew very weary, and wished to return to the house, but did not know how, and felt afraid of encountering all the strangers who would be there, unprotected by either of the Miss Brownings. Th hot sun told upon her head, and it began to ache. She saw a great wide-spreading cedar tree upon a burst of lawn towards which she was advancing, and the blank repose beneath it lured her thither. There was a rustic seat in the shadow, and weary Molly sat down there, and presently fell asleep.

*

Andrew Marvell

"The Garden" from *Miscellaneous Poems* (1681)

How vainly men themselves amaze
To win the Palm, the Oke, or Bayes;
And their incessant Labours see
Crown'd from some single Herb or Tree.
Whose short and narrow verged Shade
Does prudently their Toyles upbraid;
While all Flow'rs and all Trees do close
To weave the Garlands of repose.

Fair Quiet, have I found thee here,
And Innocence thy Sister dear!
Mistaken long, I sought you then
In busie Companies of Men.
Your sacred Plants, if here below,
Only among the plants will grow.
Society is all but rude,
To this delicious Solitude.
No white nor red was ever seen
So am'rous as this lovely green.

Fond Lovers, cruel as their Flame,
Cut in these Trees their Mistress name.
Little, Alas, they know, or heed,
How far these Beauties Hers exceed!
Fair Trees! wheresoe'er your barkes I wound,
No Name shall but your own be found.

When we have run our Passions heat,
Love hither makes his best retreat.
The *Gods*, that mortal Beauty chase,
Still in a tree did end their race.
Apollo hunted *Daphne* so,
Only that She might Laurel grow,
And *Pan* did after *Syrinx* speed,
Not as a Nymph, but for a reed.

What wond'rous life in this I lead!
Ripe Apples drop about my head;
The Luscious Clusters of the Vine
Upon my Mouth do crush their Wine;
The Nectaren, and curious Peach,
Into my hands themselves do reach;
Stumbling on Melons, as I pass,
Insnar'd with Flow'rs, I fall on Grass.

Mean while the Mind, from Pleasure less
Withdraws into its happiness:
The Mind, that Ocean where each kind
Does streight its own resemblance find;
Yet it creates, transcending these,
Far other Worlds, and other Seas;

Annihilating all that's made
To a green Thought in a green Shade.

Here at the Fountain's sliding foot,
Or at some Fruit-tree's mossy root,
Casting the Bodies Vest aside,
My Soul into the boughs does glide
Here like a bird it sits, and sings,
Then whets, and combs its silver Wings;
And till prepar'd for longer flight,
Waves in its Plumes the various Light.

Such was that happy Garden-state,
While Man there walked without a Mate:
After a Place so pure, and sweet,
What other Help could yet be meet!
But 'twas beyond a Mortal's share
To wander solitary there:
Two Paradises 'twere in one
To live in Paradise alone.

How well the skilful Gardner drew
Of flow'rs and herbes this Dial new;
Where from above the milder Sun
Does through a fragrant Zodiac run;
And, as it works, th' industrious Bee
Computes its time as well as we.
How could such sweet and wholesome Hours
Be reckon'd but with herbs and flow'rs!

LOST GARDENS

The world is full of lost gardens, and some of the most eloquent writing about gardens is about those that time or neglect has destroyed. The tone is invariably elegiac, reflecting the sadness of things that have been lost beyond the garden itself—youth, places and people we once knew and loved. The essayist William Hazlitt thinks back on the now-vanished pleasure gardens in south London where his father took him as a child, and where the bright flowers and trimmed hedges survive only in his memory. In the mind of a character in Yasunari Kawabata's novel *Beauty and Sadness*, the disarray of his Kamakura garden after the war is somehow knitted together with his concern over the absence of his son. For Alfred Lord Tennyson, the fading of a forgotten garden presages the inevitable loss of our own existence, as the passage of time erases anyone's memory of us.

John Clare is above all the poet of regret in transience. Again and again he writes with unhappiness and anger of the changes inflicted upon the countryside he knew and loved, never more vividly than when speaking of a lost childhood garden:

> The house, the dame, the garden known no more:
> While neighbouring nigh, one lonely elder tree
> Is all that's left of what had used to be.

No garden lasts forever.

William Hazlitt

"Why Distant Objects Please" from *Table-Talk: Essays on Men and Manners* (1822)

When I was quite a boy my father used to take me to the Monpelier Tea-Gardens at Walworth. Do I go there now? No, the place is deserted, and its borders and its beds are o'erturned. Is there, then, nothing that can

> 'Bring back the hour
> Of glory in the grass, of splendour in the flower?'

Oh! Yes. I unlock the casket of memory and draw back the warders of the brain; and there this scene of my infant wandering still lives unfaded, or with fresher dyes. A new sense come upon me, as in a dream; a richer perfume, brighter colours start out; my eyes dazzle, my heart heaves with its new load of bliss, and I am a child again. My sensations are all glossy, spruce, voluptuous, and fine; they wear a candied coat, and are in holiday trim. I see the beds of larkspur with purple eyes, tall holy-oaks, red and yellow; the broad sun-flowers, caked in gold, with bees buzzing round them; wildernesses of pinks and hot-glowing pionies; poppies run to seed; the sugared lily, and faint mignonette, all ranged in order, and thick as they can grow; the boxtree borders; the gravel-walks, the painted alcove, the confectioner, the clotted cream:—I think I see them now with sparkling looks; or have they vanished while I have been writing this description of them? No matter, they will return again when I least think of them. All that I have observed since, of flowers and plants, and grass-plots, of the suburban delights, seems to me borrowed from "That first garden of my innocence"—to be slips and scions stolen from that bed of memory. In this manner the darlings of our childhood burnish out in the eye of after-years, and derive their sweetest perfume from the first heartfelt sign of pleasure breathed upon them,

> 'Like the sweet south,
> That breathes upon a bank of violets,
> Stealing and giving odour.'

*

Yasunari Kawabata
Beauty and Sadness (1961)
Translated by Howard Hibbett

Oki himself began to worry about how long Taichiro had been gone.

He looked out of the small French window of his study. At the base of the hill behind the house a high mound of earth, dug out during the war in making an air raid shelter, was already hidden by weeds so modest one barely noticed them. Among the weeds bloomed a mass of flowers the colour of lapis lazuli. The flowers were extremely small, but they were a bright, strong blue. Except for the sweet daphne, these flowers bloomed earlier than any in their garden. And they stayed in bloom a long time. Whatever they were, they could hardly be familiar harbingers of spring, but they were so close to his window that he often thought he would like to take one in his hand and study it. He had never yet gone to pick one, but that seemed only to increase his love for these tiny lapis-blue flowers.

Soon after them the dandelions also came to bloom in the thickets of weeds. They were long-lived too. Even now in the fading evening light you could see the yellow of dandelions and the blue of all the little flowers. For a long time Oki looked out of the window.

Taichiro had still not come home.

*

Gustave Flaubert
Over Strand and Field (1904)

After one crosses the bridge and arrives at the steep path which leads to the Chateau [de Clisson], one sees, standing upreared and bold on the moat on which it is built, a formidable wall, crowned with battered machicolations and bedecked with trees and ivy, the luxuriant growth of which covers the grey stones and sways in the wind, like an immense green veil which the recumbent giant moves dreamily across his shoulders. The grass is tall and dark, the plants are strong and hardy; the trunks of the ivy are twisted, knotted and rough, and lift up the walls as with levers to hold them in the network of their branches. In one spot, a tree has grown through the wall horizontally, and, suspended in the air, has let its branches radiate around it. The moats, the steep slope of which is broken by the earth which has detached itself from the embankments and the stones which have fallen from the battlements, have a wide, deep curve, like hatred and pride, and the portal, with its strong, slightly arched ogive, and its two great bays that raise the drawbridge, looks like a great helmet with holes in the visor.

When one enters, he is surprised and astonished by the wonderful mixture of ruins and trees, the ruins accentuating the freshness of the trees, while the latter in turn more poignant the melancholy of the ruins. Here, indeed, is the beautiful, eternal, and brilliant laughter of nature over the skeleton of things; here is the insolence of her wealth and the deep grace of her encroachments, and the melodious invasions of her silence. A grave and pensive enthusiasm fills one's soul; one feels that the sap flows in the trees and that the grass grows with the same strength and the same rhythm, and the stones crumble and the walls cave in. A sublime art, in the supreme accord of secondary discordances, has contrasted the unruly ivy with the sinuous sweep of the ruins, the brambles with the heaps of crumbling stones, the clearness of the atmosphere with the strong projections of the masses, the colour of the sky with the colour of the earth, reflecting each one in the other; that which was, and that which is. Thus history and nature always reveal, though they may accomplish it in a circumscribed spot of the world, the unceasing relation, the eternal hymn of dying humanity and the growing daisy; of the stars that glow, and the men who expire, of the heart that beats and the waves that rise. And this is so clearly indicated here, as it is so overwhelming, that one shudders inwardly, as if this dual life centred in one's own body; so brutal and so immediate is the perception of these harmonies and developments. For the eye also has its orgies and the mind its delights.

At the foot of the large trees, the trunks of which are intersected, a stream of light floods the grass and seems like a luminous river, brightening the solitude. Overhead, a dome of leaves, through which one can see the sky presenting a vivid contrast of blue, reverberates a bright, greenish light, which illuminates the ruins, accentuating the deep furrows, intensifying the shadows, and disclosing all the hidden beauties. You advance and walk between those walls and under the trees, wander along the barbicans, pass under the falling arcades from which spring large, waving plants. The vaults, which contain corpses, echo under your footfalls; lizards run in the grass, beetles creep along the walls, the sky is blue, and the sleepy ruins pursue their dream.

✻

Alfred, Lord Tennyson
"In Memoriam" (1850)

CI

Unwatched, the garden bough shall sway,
The tender blossom flutter down,
Unloved, that beech will gather brown,
This maple burn itself away.

Unloved, the sun-flower, shining fair
Ray round with flames her disk of seed,
And many a rose-carnation feed
With summer spice the humming air;

Unloved, by many a sandy bar,
The brook shall babble down the plain,
At noon or when the lesser wain
Is twisting round the polar star;

Uncared for, gird the windy grove,
And flood the haunts of hern and crake;
Or into silver arrows break
The sailing moon in creek and cove;

Till from the garden and the wild
Afresh association blow,
And year by year the landscape grow
Familiar to the stranger's child;

As year by year the labourer tills
His wonted glebe, or lops the glades;
And year by year our memory fades
From all the circle of the hills.

*

Anne Brontë
The Tenant of Wildfell Hall (1848)

Near the top of this hill, about two miles from Linden-
Car, stood Wildfell Hall, a superannuated mansion of the
Elizabethan era, built of dark grey stone, venerable and
picturesque to look at, but doubtless, cold and gloomy
enough to inhabit, with its thick stone mullions and little
latticed panes, its time-eaten air-holes, and its too lonely,
too unsheltered situation,—only shielded from the war of
wind and weather by a group of Scotch firs, themselves half
blighted with storms, and looking as stern and gloomy as
the Hall itself. Behind it lay a few desolate fields, and then
the brown heath–clad summit of the hill; before it (enclosed

by stone walls, and entered by an iron gate, with large balls of grey granite—similar to those which decorated the roof and gables—surmounting the gate–posts) was a garden,—once stocked with such hard plants and flowers as could best brook the soil and climate, and such trees and shrubs as could best endure the gardener's torturing shears, and most readily assume the shapes he chose to give them,—now, having been left so many years untilled and untrimmed, abandoned to the weeds and the grass, to the frost and the wind, the rain and the drought, it presented a very singular appearance indeed. The close green walls of privet, that had bordered the principal walk, were two-thirds withered away, and the rest grown beyond all reasonable bounds; the old boxwood swan, that sat beside the scraper, had lost its neck and half its body: the castellated towers of laurel in the middle of the garden, the gigantic warrior that stood on one side of the gateway, and the lion that guarded the other, were sprouted into such fantastic shapes as resembled nothing either in heaven or earth, or in the waters under the earth; but, to my young imagination, they presented all of them a goblinish appearance, that harmonised well with the ghostly legions and dark traditions our old nurse had told us respecting the haunted hall and its departed occupants.

*

Frances Hodgson Burnett
The Secret Garden (1907)

She held back the swinging curtain of ivy and pushed back the door which opened slowly—slowly.

Then she slipped through it, and shut it fast behind her, and stood with her back against it, looking about her and breathing quite fast with excitement, and wonder, and delight.

She was standing inside the secret garden.

It was the sweetest, most mysterious-looking place anyone could imagine. The high walls which shut it in were covered with the leafless stems of climbing roses, which were so thick that they were matted together. Mary Lennox knew that they were roses because she had seen a great many roses in India. All the ground was covered with grass of a wintry brown, and out of it grew clumps of bushes which were surely rose-bushes if they were alive. There were numbers of standard roses which had so spread their branches that they were like little trees. There were other trees in the garden, and one of the things that made the place look strangest and loveliest was that the climbing roses had run all over them and swung down long tendrils which made light, swaying curtains, and here and there they had caught each other or at a far-reaching branch and had crept from one tree to another and made lovely bridges of themselves. There was neither leaves nor roses on them now, and Mary did not know whether they were dead or alive, but their thin grey or brown branches and sprays looked like a sort of hazy mantle spreading over everything, walls, and trees, and even brown grass, where they had fallen from their fastenings and run along the ground. It was this hazy tangle from tree to tree which made it look so mysterious. Mary had thought it must be different from other gardens which had not been left all by themselves for so long; and, indeed, it was different from any other place she had ever seen in her life.

*

John Clare
"The Cross Roads; or, The Haymaker's Story"
(First published in 1921)

> And where majoram once, and sage, and rue,
> And balm, and mint, and curled-leaf parsley grew,
> And double marigolds, and silver thyme,
> And pumpkins neath the window used to climb;
> And where I often when a child for hours
> Tried through the pales to get the tempting flowers,
> As lady's laces, everlasting peas,
> True-love-lies-bleeding, with the hearts-at-ease,
> And golden rods, and tansy running high
> That oer the pale-tops smiled on passers-by,
> Flowers in my time that everyone would praise,
> Though thrown like weeds from gardens nowadays;
> Where all these grew, now henbane stinks and spreads,
> And docks and thistles shake their seedy heads,
> And yearly keep with nettles smothering oer;—
> The house, the dame, the garden known no more:
> While neighbouring nigh, one lonely elder tree
> Is all that's left of what had used to be.

WHO'S WHO

Louisa May Alcott 1832–1888 American novelist best known for
Little Women

John Aubrey 1626–1697 Antiquary and famously uninhibited
biographer in his *Brief Lives*

Jane Austen 1775–1817 Author of half a dozen of the most
delightful novels in the English language

Honoré de Balzac 1799–1850 French writer of the great group of
interconnected novels known as the *Comédie Humaine*

Giovanni Boccaccio 1313–1375 Florentine writer and scholar
whose chief work was the collection of stories known as
The Decameron

James Boswell 1740–1795 Author of the first great modern
biography, of Samuel Johnson

Elizabeth Bowen 1899–1973 Anglo-Irish novelist and short-story
writer. Her best-known novels are *The Death of the Heart* and
The Heat of the Day

Anne Brontë 1820–1849 Sister of Charlotte and Emily Brontë and like them the author of novels, though with less success

Charlotte Brontë 1816–1855 Eldest and most-admired of the Brontë sisters, author of *Jane Eyre*. *Villette* draws upon her experiences as a student in Brussels in the 1840s

Sir Thomas Browne 1605–1682 Doctor and writer, great literary stylist

Robert Burton 1577–1640 Author of *The Anatomy of Melancholy*, an enormous compendium of anecdotes and maxims masquerading as a medical text

Robert Byron 1905–1940 Distinguished travel writer and expert on Byzantine art and architecture whose most memorable book is *The Road to Oxiana*

Cao Xueqin 1715–1763 Chinese author what is probably the greatest novel in that language, *The Dream of the Red Chamber* (also available in English as *The Story of the Stone*), not published until thirty years after his death

Karel Čapek 1890–1938 Czech playwright, journalist and gardener, author of *R.U.R.* and *The Makropulos Secret*, as well as several novels and wonderfully funny books on gardening

Emily Carr 1871–1945 Canadian painter who also wrote several largely autobiographical novels

Willa Cather 1876–1947 American novelist, most of whose work is set in the Midwest

Anton Chekhov 1860–1904 Russian dramatist and short story writer who trained as a doctor and became author of a number of powerful plays still frequently produced

John Clare 1793–1864 Born the son of a farm labourer and poor countryman himself, his poetry celebrates fast-vanishing rural ways and mourns their passing. He went mad; much of his work was not published until after his death

Colette 1873–1954 French novelist known only by her surname (her given names were Sidonie Gabrielle) whose works are especially noted for their sensitivity to nature and to the psychology of women

Joseph Conrad 1857–1924 Anglicized Polish sea captain (born Teodor Josef Konrad Korzeniowski) who turned to writing novels when he was nearly 40, producing a number of masterly works including *Lord Jim* and *Nostromo*

e e cummings 1864–1962 American poet whose work often displayed unusual typography along with remarkable lyric power, and famously preferred to lower-case his own name

Alphonse Daudet 1840–1897 French author of many novels, best known for his sketches of Provençal life, though *Fromont and Risler* is set in Paris

Walter de la Mare 1873–1956 Poet, novelist and short story writer, whose many books included a number for children

Prince Charles-Joseph de Ligne 1735–1814 Austrian military officer and writer, author of books on war and tactics, as well as stories and a fascinating account of his estate and its gardens, *Coup d'oeil sur Beloeil*

Mary Delany 1700–1788 Friend and correspondent of Jonathan Swift, member of the circle of female writers known as Blue Stockings

Charles Dickens 1812–1870 Enormously successful author of many wonderful novels that received critical as well as popular acclaim

Benjamin Disraeli 1804–1881 Politician, prime minister and novelist, a wholly extraordinary man and prolific writer. 'When I want to read a novel,' he once said, 'I will write one'.

John Donne 1572–1631 Late-blooming clergyman and celebrated preacher, he became dean of St Paul's and is now regarded as the finest non-dramatic poet of his time

Alexandre Dumas 1802–1870 Known as Dumas *père* to distinguish him from his similarly named son, author of highly popular mostly historical novels including *The Three Musketeers* and *The Count of Monte Cristo*

George Eliot 1819–1880 Pen name of Mary Ann (later Marian) Evans, who wrote some of the best novels of the Victorian era— *Middlemarch, Adam Bede, The Mill on the Floss* among others

D. J. Enright 1920–2002 Poet and essayist, spent many years teaching in the Far East where many of his poems are set

Henry Fielding 1707–1754 Judge, dramatist, brilliant satirist, and author of some of the funniest and most readable novels of the eighteenth century, including *The History of Tom Jones*

F. Scott Fitzgerald 1896–1940 American writer. Best novel probably *The Great Gatsby*, though *Tender is the Night*, a story about a psychiatrist and his schizophrenic wife, is memorable too

Gustave Flaubert 1821–1880 Supreme French stylist, author of *Madame Bovary* and a number of other highly-regarded novels

E. M. Forster 1879–1970 Retiring novelist and short story writer, best-known for *A Passage to India* and *A Room with a View*, both of which have been filmed

John Galsworthy 1867–1933 Popular Edwardian playwright and novelist (*The Forsyte Saga*) now fallen rather out of fashion

John Galt 1779–1839 Scottish writer known for his fictional studies of country life in his native land

Elizabeth Gaskell 1810–1865 With George Eliot, now considered one of the major figures in nineteenth century English fiction with *Cranford, North and South,* and *Wives and Daughters*

Johann Wolfgang von Goethe 1749–1832 Most famous for his two-part poem *Faust,* he was the leading figure in the German literary renaissance. In the novel *Elective Affinities* he deals in a subtle and modern way with the attraction of a married couple to two other persons

Nikolai Gogol 1809–1852 Russian story writer, dramatist and savage satirist, author of *The Government Inspector, Dead Souls* and other powerfully imaginative works

Thom Gunn 1929–2004 Poet born in England who settled in San Francisco; his verse combines the laconic rational manner of the English Modern Movement with the unbridled romantic content of the American Beat poets

Robert Harbison 1940– American cultural and architectural historian whose brilliantly original book *Eccentric Spaces* explores the interplay between the human imagination and the places we create to live in

Nathaniel Hawthorne 1804–1864 American author of an array of classic short stories and novels, from *The Scarlet Letter* to *Twice-told Tales*

William Hazlitt 1778–1830 Prolific essayist, critic and journeyman writer

Lafcadio Hearn 1850–1904 Eminently international writer: born in Greece, educated in England, émigré in the United States and Matinique, ultimately settled in Japan, about which he wrote several books

Robert Heath c. 1620–1685 or after Minor Caroline poet, author of a few lyrics and poems on Civil War battles

John Hollander 1929– Prizewinning American poet and professor, author of more than two dozen books of verse and criticism

Homer Dates unknown, perhaps eighth century BC Supposed author of the two most famous works of Greek epic poetry, the *Iliad* and the *Odyssey*

William Dean Howells 1837–1920 Editor, critic and novelist, a leading figure on the late nineteenth American literary scene; author of *The Rise of Silas Lapham* and *A Hazard of New Fortunes* among other works

Constantijn Huygens 1596–1687 Dutch diplomat and poet, a major player in the Dutch Renaissance, designer of a magnificent house and garden near the Hague about which he wrote a descriptive poem

Washington Irving 1783–1859 American satirist and journalist ('Rip van Winkle', 'The Legend of Sleepy Hollow' and other tales and essays)

James I of Scotland 1394–1437 A literary king, with several works attributed to him including *The Kingis Quair*

Henry James 1843–1916 American novelist renowned for his labyrinthine sentences and psychological subtlety in *Portrait of a Lady, Wings of the Dove, The Golden Bowl* and others

Jerome K. Jerome 1859–1927 Journalist and humorous essayist who achieved lasting comic fame with *Three Men in a Boat*

Samuel Johnson 1709–1784 The Great Cham: lexicographer, essayist, talker, memorialized (and immortalized) by James Boswell in his classic biography

Yasunari Kawabata 1899–1972 A key figure in the school of modern Japanese fiction with such novels as *The Sound of the Mountain* and *Snow Country,* winner of the 1968 Nobel Prize

Sir Robert Ker Porter 1777–1842 Painter and traveler, author of fine atmospheric accounts of his journeys

Rudyard Kipling 1865–1936 Storyteller and poet, author of books for children (*Kim, The Jungle Book*) and adults as well as a great deal of fluent and unforgettable verse

Giuseppe Tomasi di Lampedusa 1896–1957 Sicilian nobleman, author of a single marvelous novel, *The Leopard,* about the social and political upheaval following Garibaldi's takeover of Sicily in 1860

D. H. Lawrence 1885–1930 Best-known for his novel *Lady Chatterley's Lover,* he courted controversy through most of his career, writing powerful fiction and evocative, sometimes eccentric, travel books

Edward Lear 1812–1888 Excellent painter and superlative writer of nonsense verses that are not necessarily funny

Lu You 1125–1210 Prolific poet of the Southern Song Dynasty, retired to the countryside after an unsuccessful government career

Percy Lubbock 1879–1965 Biographer (*Portrait of Edith Wharton*), critic and memoirist whose *Earlham* describes his own childhood days in Norfolk

Gervase Markham 1568–1637 Writer on country pursuits, hunting, horsemanship and military tactics, as well as husbandry

Andrew Marvell 1621–1678 Brilliant poet and satirist who was virtually forgotten for two centuries after his death but has now been restored to a high place in critical admiration

William Mason 1725–1795 Poet of modest gifts whose long poem *The English Garden* makes plain his admiration for the new picturesque style of landscape design

Somerset Maugham 1874–1965 Successful playwright and novelist (*Of Human Bondage, The Moon and Sixpence, Cakes and Ale*) who never received much critical acclaim; of himself he said he had a place 'in the very first row of second-raters'

William Maxwell 1908–2000 Long-time American fiction editor of the *New Yorker* and author of six beautifully-wrought novels and many short stories

Mary Russell Mitford 1787–1855 Distinguished letter-writer and dramatist best remembered for her collection of stories and essays *Our Village*

L. M. Montgomery 1874–1942 Much-loved Canadian author of the series of seven children's books beginning with *Anne of Green Gables*, set on Prince Edward Island, and many others

John Parkinson 1567–1650 Herbalist and writer; his punningly entitled *Paradisi in sole Paradisus terrestris, or a garden of all sorts of pleasant flowers which our English ayre will permit to be noursed up* [etc] is his masterwork and one of the most important early gardening manuals

Thomas Love Peacock 1785–1866 Profoundly funny satirist of contemporary foibles, including the fad for large-scale landscape design

Samuel Pepys 163–1703 Possibly the best diarist of all time—civil servant, womanizer, a man intensely engaged with life

Bo Juyi *or* **Po Chü-I** The most famous poet of the Tang Dynasty, partly because he is the easiest to read; like many poets of the period his themes tend to be regret and nostalgia

Alexander Pope 1688–1744 A skilled and critically important poet in many modes from didactic to lyric, he was also a tastemaker in such matters as garden design

Marcel Proust 1871–1922 One novel—but what a novel! *A la recherché du temps perdu* (published in English as *Remembrance of Things Past*) took him his whole life to write, but stands unparalleled for its ground-breaking intricacy and psychological precision

Sir Walter Scott 1771–1832 Father of the romantic novel, storyteller par excellence in such books as *Heart of Midlothian* and *Old Mortality*. Gardener and tree-planter

Sei Shōnagon c.966–1017 Japanese court lady, author of the delightful rag-bag of stories, observations, gossip and jokes known as *The Pillow Book*

Thomas Sheridan 1687–1738 Irish wit, churchman and intimate friend of Jonathan Swift. Author of an abundance of satirical mostly light verse, and grandfather of the famous playwright and politician Richard Brinsley Sheridan

James Shirley 1596–1666 Author of some forty plays and masques who chose the wrong side in the Civil War and ended a schoolmaster

Sir Osbert Sitwell 1892–1969 Prolific writer of poems, fiction and travel books, plus a five-volume autobiography

Sir George Sitwell 1863–1943 Highly eccentric baronet, father of Osbert (and Edith and Sacheverell), expert on garden design who restored and developed gardens in Italy and at the family estate of Renishaw Hall in Derbyshire

Tobias Smollett 1721–1771 Powerful and effective satirist in verse and prose, author of several important picaresque novels including *Humphrey Clinker, Roderick Random,* and *Peregrine Pickle*

Robert Southey 1774–1843 Critic and author of a vast amount of poetry and journalism who became Poet Laureate in 1813 and hated it

Laurence Sterne 1713–1768 Clergyman who found fame as a writer only in middle age with his nine-volume shaggy-dog novel *Tristram Shandy*

Robert Louis Stevenson 1850–1894 Beset by poor health during much of his life he nevertheless wrote verse and stories for children and a number of entertaining (and sometimes serious) novels for adults

Tom Stoppard 1937– Dramatist responsible for many highly successful plays (*The Real Inspector Hound, Rosencrantz and Guildenstern are dead, Travesties, Arcadia*)

Sir Roy Strong 1935– Art historian and museum director (National Portrait Gallery, V & A), writer, creator of a magnificent garden at his house in Herefordshire

Su Shi 1037–1101 Leading Song Dynasty poet, also famed for his calligraphy and paintings

Tanizaki Junichirō 1886–1965 Japanese novelist whose work intertwines Eastern and Western themes; one of the most important and popular modern Japanese writers with such books as *The Makioka Sisters, Some Prefer Nettles,* and *The Key*

Sir William Temple 1628–1699 Diplomat and enthusiastic gardener, author of essays and memoirs

Alfred Lord Tennyson 1809–1892 Grand Old Man of Victorian poetry whose works (*In Memoriam, Maud, Idylls of the King*) enjoyed great popularity but fell from favor later

Flora Thompson 1876–1947 Best-remembered for her auto-biographical trilogy *Lark Rise to Candleford* about growing up in a now-vanished rural world in the Oxfordshire countryside

William Trevor 1928– Anglo-Irish author of many poignant and keenly-observed novels and short stories, mostly set in Ireland

Anthony Trollope 1815–1882 Writer and Post Office executive, author of no fewer than 47 novels, plus many volumes of short stories, travel books, and autobiography

Ivan Turgenev 1818–1883 Russian novelist and playwright who spent most of his life abroad where he was widely acquainted with leading literary figures; the first Russian novelist to gain a reputation and exert influence outside his native country

Mark Twain (Samuel Clemens) 1835–1910 American humorist, travel writer, novelist (*Huckleberry Finn, Tom Sawyer*) who delighted in skewering the pretensions of his compatriots

Elizabeth von Arnim 1866–1941 Australian who married a German count and moved to Pomerania, where she lived not altogether happily and created a garden, writing a book about it

Horace Walpole 1717–1797 Dilettante connoisseur, writer, garden designer, tastemaker, one of the very finest letter-writers who ever lived

Charles Dudley Warner 1829–1900 American newspaper editor and essayist, author of one of the most delightful of all gardening books *My Summer in a Garden*

Eudora Welty 1909–2001 Pulitzer Prize-winning novelist and short story writer known for her sometimes gothic imagination; most of her work is set in the American South

Edith Wharton 1862–1937 Born to wealth and unhappily married, made her career as a leading American novelist and short story writer (*The Custom of the Country, The Age of Innocence, Hudson River Bracketed, The House of Mirth*) mainly after her divorce

Patrick White 1912–1990 Australian novelist, author of *Tree of Man* and *Voss* among many profound and highly-regarded books; won Nobel Prize in 1973

Mary Wollstonecraft 1759–1797 Wrote one novel (*Mary*) but much better known for her influential *A Vindication of the Rights of Women*; mother of Mary Shelley

Virginia Woolf 1882–1941 One of the most important and original novelists of the modern era, pioneer in the use of 'stream of consciousness' and other innovations; author of such works as *Mrs Dalloway, To the Lighthouse* and *Orlando* as well as many delightful essays

William Wordsworth 1770–1850 A radical and innovator early in his career, gradually became more conventional as his poetry achieved fame and wide popularity; works include *The Prelude, Lyrical Ballads* (with Coleridge), *The Excursion* and many others, both narrative and lyric

SOURCES & ACKNOWLEDGMENTS

INDEX

A

"Advice, The" 52
Alcott, Louisa May 45, 180
Anatomy of Melancholy, The
    29, *181*
Anne of Green Gables 20, 187
Arcadia 37, 44, 189
Aubrey, John 71, 180
Austen, Jane 88, 112, 180
Awkward Age, The 12, 30

B

Balzac, Honoré de 15, 156, 180
Beatrix 15
Beauty and Sadness 169, 172
Black Tulip, The 124, 128
Bleak House 79
Boccaccio, Giovanni 34, 180

Boswell, James 37, 67, 180,
    185
Bowen, Elizabeth 10, 112, 180
Brontë, Anne 176, 181
Brontë, Charlotte 10, 140, 142,
    181
Browne, Sir Thomas 91, 98,
    181
Burton, Robert 29, 181
Byron, Robert 93, 181

C

Cao Xueqin 92, 96, 181
Čapek, Karel 38, 181
Carr, Emily 70, 87, 181
Cather, Willa 124, 136, 181
Celebration of Gardens, A 73
Chateau, The 127

Chekhov, Anton 116, 181
Clare, John 123, 135, 170,
     179, 181
Colette 13, 17, 52, 182
Conrad, Joseph 132, 182
Country Farm 48
Country House, The 49
Coup d'Oeil at Beloeil 61, 182
Cummings, e e 7, 182

D

Daudet, Alphonse 58, 182
De la Mare, Walter 35, 182
De Ligne, Prince Charles-
     Joseph 61, 182
Dead Souls 147, 184
Decameron, The 34, 180
Delany, Mary 115, 182
Diary 66
Dickens, Charles 79, 182
Disraeli, Benjamin 12, 13, 182
Doctor &c, The 107
Donne, John 153, 163, 183
Dream of the Red Chamber 96,
     181
"Dreary Story, A" 116
Dumas, Alexandre 124, 128,
     183

E

Earlham 32, 186
Eccentric Spaces 143, 184
"Eight Poems of the Eastern
     Slope" 63
Elective Affinities 37, 65, 184
Eliot, George 124, 126, 183
Elizabeth Alone 120
*Elizabeth and Her German
     Garden 80*
"English Garden, The" 113,
     186
Enright, D. J. 101, 183
"Epistle to Burlington" 64
*Essay on the Making of
     Gardens 133*
Eugénie Grandet 156
Eye of the Storm, The 161

F

Fielding, Henry 85, 183
Fitzgerald, F. Scott 91, 103,
     183
Flaubert, Gustave 173, 183
Forster, E. M. 76, 183

G

Galsworthy, John 49, 183
Galt, John 89, 183
"Garden of the Gods, The"
     159

Gardener's Year, The 39
Gardens of Cyrus, The 98
Gaskell, Elizabeth 153, 164, 183
Glimpses of Unfamiliar Japan 99
"Glory of the Garden, The" 74
Goethe, Johann Wolfgang von 10, 37, 65, 184
Gogol, Nikolai 10, 147, 184
Gunn, Thom 159, 184

H

Harbison, Robert 143, 184
Hawthorne, Nathaniel 141, 149, 184
Hazlitt, William 169, 171, 184
Headlong Hall 37, 42
Hearn, Lafcadio 91, 99, 184
Heath, Robert 16, 184
Henrietta Temple 14
History of Tom Jones, The 85, 183
Hofwijk 60
Hollander, John 50, 184
Homer 10, 101, 185
House of All Sorts, The 87
House of Gentlefolk, A 78
Howard's End 76
Howells, William Dean 23, 185

Humphrey Clinker 72, 188
Huygens, Constantin 38, 60, 185

I

"Ideal House, The" 40
"In Memoriam" 175, 189
Indian Summer 23
Innocent Libertine, The 17
Innocents Abroad 111
"Instructions to the Landscaper" 50
Irving, Washington 124, 132, 185

J

James I of Scotland 10, 12, 19, 185
James, Henry 12, 30, 185
Jerome, Jerome K. 10, 106, 117, 185
Johnson, Samuel 10, 37, 67, 105, 107, 140, 146, 180, 185

K

Kawabata, Yasunari 169, 172, 185
Ker Porter, Sir Robert 91, 94, 185
"Kew Gardens" 10, 154, 157
Kingis Quair, The 19, 185

Kipling, Rudyard 74, 186
"Kyoto Garden, A" 101

L

Lampedusa, Giuseppe Tomasi
   di 140, 147, 186
Lark Rise to Candleford 124,
   138, 189
Last of the Lairds, The 89
Lawrence, D. H. 140, 145, 186
Lear, Edward 69, 71, 186
Leopard, The 140, 147, 186
Letters to Montagu 46, 155
Letters Written during a
   Residence in Sweden 114
Life of Samuel Johnson, The 67
Little Women 45, 180
Lives of the Poets, The 107
Lu You 94, 186
Lubbock, Percy 32, 186

M

Magician, The 115
Makioka Sisters, The 100, 189
Mansfield Park 112
Markham, Gervase 48, 186
Marvell, Andrew 10, 153, 166,
   186
Mason, William 105, 113, 186
Maugham, Somerset 10, 115,
   186

Maxwell, William 127, 187
Mitford, Mary Russell 84, 187
Montgomery, L. M. 20, 187
"Moor Park" 105
My Summer in a Garden 58,
   190

N

Natural History of Wiltshire,
   The 71
Nostromo 132, 182

O

Odyssey 101, 91, 185
"On Clarastella Walking in her
   Garden" 16
"On Hawkstone Park" 146
Over Strand and Field 173

P

Paradisi in Sole Paradisus
   Terrestris 53, 187
Parkinson, John 10, 53, 187
Peacock, Thomas Love 37, 42,
   187
Penny Foolish 51
Pepys, Samuel 66, 187
"Phantoms" 151
Pillow Book, The 10, 160, 188
"Planting Flowers by the
   Eastern Embankment" 83

Plumed Serpent, The 140, 145

Po Chü-I 83, 187

Pope, Alexander 10, 38, 64, 70, 82, 187

Pride and Prejudice 88

Professor's House, The 136

Proust, Marcel 13, 27, 187

R

"Rappaccini's Daughter" 141, 149

Remembrance of Things Past 27, 187

S

Scenes of Clerical Life 124, 126

Scott, Sir Walter 21, 188

Sei Shōnagon 10, 154, 160, 188

Sheridan, Thomas 88

Shirley, James 56, 188

"Shoes" 112

Sitwell, Osbert 51, 188

Sitwell, Sir George 10, 123, 133, 188

Sketch Book, The 124, 132

"Small Garden" 94

Small House at Allington, The 105, 114

Smollett, Tobias 72, 109, 188

Southey, Robert 107, 188

Sterne, Laurence 54, 188

Stevenson, Robert Louis 38, 40, 189

Stoppard, Tom 37, 44, 189

Strong, Sir Roy 70, 73, 189

Su Shi 38, 63, 189

"Sunken Garden, The" 35

T

Tanizaki, Junichirō 100, 189

Temple, Sir William 76, 105, 189

Tenant of Wildfell Hall, The 176

Tender is the Night 103, 183

Tennyson, Alfred Lord 169, 175, 181

"This is the Garden" 7

Thompson, Flora 124, 138, 189

Three Men in a Boat 106, 117, 185

Travels in Georgia 94

Travels through France and Italy 109

Trevor, William 120, 189

Tristram Shandy 54, 188

Trollope, Anthony 105, 114, 189

Turgenev, Ivan 78, 151, 190

Twain, Mark 105, 111, 190
"Twicknam Garden" 163

V

Valley of Decision, The 25
Villette 140, 142, 181
Von Arnim, Elizabeth 80, 190

W

Walpole, Horace 46, 155, 190
Warner, Charles Dudley 58,
    190
Waverley 21
Welty, Eudora 154, 155
Wharton, Edith 25, 186, 190
"White Doe of Rylestone, The"
    81
White, Patrick 161, 190
"Why Distant Objects Please"
    171
Wives and Daughters 164, 183
Wollstonecraft, Mary 106, 114,
    190
Woolf, Virginia 10, 154, 157,
    191
Wordsworth, William 81, 191